About the Author

The author is a rabbi and practicing attorney. He and his wife, children and grandchildren live in the Eye of the Universe — Jerusalem.

The Beach Boy

William Semenow

The Beach Boy

Olympia Publishers
London

www.olympiapublishers.com
OLYMPIA PAPERBACK EDITION

Copyright © William Semenow 2022

The right of William Semenow to be identified as author of this work has been asserted in accordance with sections 77 and 78 of the Copyright, Designs and Patents Act 1988.

All Rights Reserved

No reproduction, copy or transmission of this publication may be made without written permission.
No paragraph of this publication may be reproduced, copied or transmitted save with the written permission of the publisher, or in accordance with the provisions of the Copyright Act 1956 (as amended).

Any person who commits any unauthorised act in relation to this publication may be liable to criminal prosecution and civil claims for damage.

A CIP catalogue record for this title is available from the British Library.

ISBN: 978-1-80074-105-8

First Published in 2022

Olympia Publishers
Tallis House
2 Tallis Street
London
EC4Y 0AB

Printed in Great Britain

Dedication

This book is dedicated to the memory of my parents, grandparents and great-grandparents. May they continually ascend to the highest heights in Heaven and may their descendants always be a credit to their names.

Acknowledgements

It is unlikely that this book would ever have been written without the example shown to me by my good friend, Dr Zalman Frist. As a legacy for his family, he had undertaken the writing of an autobiography and sent me an early draft.

I had always been interested in family history and even as a little boy had asked my parents, grandparents and other close relations about their lives and recollections. Over the years I have told some of the stories I have heard from them to my children, but not too many to my grandchildren. At some point in the future, I imagine that at least some of them will want to know where they came from, as I did. I never thought of reducing that history to book form until Zalman showed me his manuscript.

While I had begun this project before the coronavirus pandemic, progress was slow. I didn't have much time for writing. But with the corona lockdowns I now had much more time to write. So, in a perverse way, I must acknowledge the pandemic's contribution to this book.

I greatly appreciate the help that my brother, Yaacov Meyer, has given me with his own recollections and his ability to retrieve old photographs and recording tapes, which would have otherwise been lost.

I appreciate the encouragement from my sister, Deena Rochel, and my children who have read either the whole or parts of the manuscript. Without their encouragement, I might have abandoned the project altogether.

I also wish to thank Dr Adam Levine and Mrs Helena Stern who read the final draft and made many valuable suggestions and corrections.

Lastly, I wish to thank my wife, Rus Chana, for her endless love, continuous encouragement and belief in me. She has been and continues to be a true *ezer c'negdo* (helpmate).

Preface

This book is autobiographical. All the facts are true as I remember them. I have changed the names of many of the individuals to protect their identities. Any similarity of their names to anyone living or dead is entirely coincidental.

Introduction
Superpowers

Did you ever wonder how kids born with superpowers discover that they're different from everyone else? Let me tell you. They don't. At least I didn't. Not for a long time anyway.

    I attribute that partly to the fact that I was a shy kid and not a show off. Had I been outgoing and showy, my parents probably would have noticed my superpowers right away and I would have been in all the newspapers and magazines and on TV and in the movies. Fortunately for me, being the shy type, I wasn't subjected to fame until I was much older and for reasons unrelated to my superpowers. But that's for later.

    You probably don't believe me. I mean, if someone had told me that he had superpowers, I wouldn't believe him. I'm a natural skeptic. First, I'd assume he was a liar. Then, I would assume that what he calls superpowers are actually normal human abilities but because he thinks he performs them well, they're superpowers. Take a kid who runs fast. He might think he's faster than anyone in the world and that he's actually the possessor of a superpower. But, in reality, he can just beat his three slow friends in a race around the block. And if he persisted in his insistence on his superpowers, I'd ask for a demonstration — unless it involved a life-threatening action. Like when I was six. There was a story about an eight-year-old kid in New York City who thought he could fly like

Superman. His friends dared him to show them. So, he went up to the top of his apartment house with a sheet for a cape and jumped off. Needless to say, he couldn't fly and fell twenty-five storeys to his death. I would never ask for a demonstration like that. I'd just assume the kid was nuts. So, why do I say I was born with superpowers? Because I was. Some of them were physical powers — like breathing underwater and being able to see people and objects thousands of miles away. Others relate to the ability to see problems in the universe and develop theories to explain them.

When I was very young, I was unaware that I was different from anyone else. I thought everyone could do the things I could do. Later on, I realized I was unique. But by that time, I didn't tell anyone about my superpowers, because I had developed a sense of morality and propriety and bragging wasn't either. So, I kept my secrets to myself.

Chapter 1
Assumptions

My childhood world was very egocentric, and that's as it should be. As a child who thought about the world around me, my limited experiences led me to generalize them into theories, which for the most part, I kept to myself. They did not necessarily stand the test of time.

As a child of five or six, I assumed that all people in the world understood English. It was the language I thought in. So, naturally, did everyone else. If so, how was it that people from other countries spoke different languages? Of course, they translated from the English! Although I recognized that this would be a cumbersome process, that was my conclusion. They would think, "I want a glass of water" and translate this into Spanish and say, "Quiero un vaso de agua". Why did they do this? I didn't have a good answer and it never occurred to me to ask anyone else. If I didn't know, I assumed no one else would. I guessed that they did this to preserve their cultural identity. I mean, a Frenchman speaking English in France like a New Yorker would detract from his 'Frenchness'.

I also had a theory that Jews liked chocolate and *goyim* (non-Jews) liked vanilla. I liked chocolate and so did my mother and little brother. I didn't know many *goyim* and the few I knew were at school and the Good Humor ice cream man couldn't come into the schoolyard. I don't remember having any *goyishe* friends until I was ten. I knew that vanilla was a popular flavor. So, who could be buying this tasteless stuff? I assumed it must be the *goyim*. My father preferred vanilla. And that bothered me because I was pretty sure that he was Jewish.

In third grade geography we learnt about the African Continent. In those days, Africa was colonial. A European country owned every country except for Egypt and maybe one or two others. The Belgian Congo was, I think, the largest country on the continent. I asked my teacher why the Belgians (whose European country I knew was tiny) didn't move to the Congo so that they could live in a big place. After all, who wouldn't want to move out of their small apartment (like the one I lived in) and move to a mansion? Her answer was unsatisfying. So, what if the climate was very hot? That wasn't so bad. Who liked winter anyway? And if it was primitive and undeveloped, all you had to do was build it up. Seemed like a fairly simple calculation to me.

I also believed that a mourner for one's parent had to wear a box on his back for a year. I attended the Shabbos Youth services every week at Temple Israel and one of the teenagers was saying *Kaddish* (a prayer for the dead) for his father. He had a back brace — a prosthetic device that I was unfamiliar with. It protruded from the back of his shirt, and it looked to me like he had a box strapped to his back. I assumed that he had to wear it as a symbol of mourning. It made sense to me. He was carrying on his back the burden of having a dead father — both figuratively and literally. That remained my assumption for many years. If I saw a mourner without the box, I assumed he wasn't as religious as that boy.

I assumed that the population of the United States was close to fifty percent Jewish. I lived in Long Beach, New York, a city with a majority of Jews. My parents told me that Long Beach was the only city in the United States that could claim that distinction. How Jewish was Long Beach? Every one of my friends was Jewish. And I had a lot of friends. All my relatives were Jewish My parents' and grandparents' friends were Jewish and they had many friends. In fact, pretty much everyone I knew was Jewish. With all the Jews in Long Beach and all the Jewish neighborhoods scattered throughout the New York Metropolitan area, where my cousins and aunts and uncles lived, I assumed that while perhaps other cities had a majority of non-Jews, the Jewish population of America couldn't be that far behind.

How Jewish was Long Beach? After I learned to read, I looked through our bookcase in the living room and found a book with the name Elinor Cohen written on the inside flap. My grandparents' family name was Farenthal, and my mother's name was Elinor. I asked my mother who Elinor Cohen was. She told me that it was her name. Shortly after they moved from the Bronx to Long Beach, the mailman, who was of course Jewish, complained to my grandfather that people were constantly misspelling his last name on letters addressed to him. "What are you," he said. "A Cohen, Levi or Yisrael?

"I'm a Cohen," answered my grandfather.

"Then do us all a favor and change your name to Cohen." And that's what he did. His brothers, who didn't live in Long Beach, were annoyed with his decision and after a year or two he changed it back to Farenthal.

While I had heard of anti-Semitism from my family, neighbors and the Jewish radio programs we listened to on

Sunday mornings, I never experienced it as a young child and assumed that it was a thing of the past in America. I was proud to be a Jew. In fact, I counted myself lucky and still do, that despite almost impossible odds I was born a Jew, a firstborn son whose mother was a bas Cohen (the daughter of a Cohen) and a Litvak!

Chapter 2
Long Beach

The part of Long Beach in which we lived in the fifties had very few new homes. Most were built in the early aughts of the twentieth century when Long Beach was a booming summer resort. Many were three storey buildings that were broken down into three or more apartments. Ours was one of those. My grandparents (Momma and Poppy) lived on the bottom floor, we lived on the second floor, and my great grandmother, Nani Nani, lived on the third floor. Nowadays most people in the States don't live in multigenerational dwellings but in my youth, it was common — at least in my neighborhood. It was very comforting to know that if my parents yelled at me, I could go downstairs and get sympathy from Momma and Poppy. Poppy was usually around on Saturday to play ball with me or take me to the city. I could also count on them if I didn't like the dinner that my mother made. My grandparents had a maid, Emma, who was very accommodating and would cook up whatever I fancied.

Emma was a part of our family, or to be more precise, she belonged to our family. She lived with my grandparents and worked for them until the time of their deaths. She then lived with us and after my mother took ill and had to be hospitalized, she moved in with my great aunt Ernestine on the Upper East Side. Upon my great aunt's demise, she wrote to my brother and me asking us for money. Since she worked 'off the books', she didn't qualify for social security benefits. We knew she had a daughter who was a public-school teacher in LA and whose husband was a lawyer. When we were young, she would show us pictures of their fancy house, fancy cars and swimming pool in Brentwood. She was very proud of their accomplishments, but apparently, they didn't think it was their responsibility to support her. Or maybe they helped, but it wasn't enough. Emma was born in North Carolina and came north as a young woman to work as a housemaid. Her parents were born as free people, but her grandparents had been slaves. Slavery was not an ancient institution when I was young. It had ended less than ninety years before. Thinking back on it now, it seems to me that slavery in America hadn't really ended with the North's victory in the Civil War. In fact, parts of it survived through my childhood even in the North and in liberal New York. The only difference I can think of is that Emma got a small salary to cook and clean and look after the masters and their children.

Chapter 3
Elementary School

When I was four years old my mother took me to public school to register. I remember that day. I felt so grown up. Until then I had been in nursery school in some old women's basement. I didn't like the nursery school. It was dark and damp. If we misbehaved, Mrs Black told us that she would lock us up in a darker room in the basement. She called it the 'Dungeon'. I was sufficiently frightened never to cross her. But it wasn't all bad. I did make some friends. We were given Graham crackers and milk for our daily snack. To this day I am not fond of Graham crackers and associate them with damp, dark basements.

Registration for elementary school was on Arbor Day — the last Friday in April. I don't know if it's still celebrated, but in the early fifties Arbor Day was a big deal. All the kids in the school were outside planting trees. I was dressed up in my best clothes and was given a lollipop after registering. I was happy that I was going to start school there in September. The school was above ground and there was bright daylight in the classrooms. I loved my elementary school.

PS 1, also known as 'Central School', was almost entirely Jewish. There were some non-Jews, but very few and most were Catholic. I didn't realize it at the time but, most likely the only reason they were in a public school was that they were uneducable and uncontrollable and Long Beach Catholic School had thrown them out. It would be years before I realized that Catholics could be normal and intelligent. One of the Catholics in my class, Crazy Albert, would eat anything — rocks, glass, metal. He was very entertaining but like someone from another planet. I didn't know any Protestants, although I knew they existed elsewhere in the United States, but not in any place near me. I had no assumptions about them.

Actually, that's not quite true. There were Negroes that lived in Long Beach. We had a few in our school. They were Protestants. But when I thought of Protestants, I didn't think of them.

In those days, Black people were a ghost nation. They were totally segregated and lived in rickety apartment buildings near the railroad tracks. I would guess that most of the Black women worked as domestics in the white people's houses. Everyone I knew had a Black maid. I don't remember the Black men. I suppose there were some but like our maid Emma's husband, Bill, they rarely lived at home.

Central School was a ten-minute walk from my house. And in good weather I walked to school every day through the back alleys where the Negroes lived. Although the ghetto was run down, the delicious smell of coffee brewing and discarded coffee grinds was something to look forward to. There was no fear of being attacked or robbed. In those days, at least in Long Beach, no Black would ever dream of assaulting a white kid on his way to school. My brother, Jimmy, called them the 'chocolate people' which was a better description of their color than Negro or Black and also made them sound sweet and tasty.

It seemed to me that my mother knew every teacher and

secretary in the school. Having grown up in Long Beach, she probably knew every Jew in town and many of her friends became the teachers in my school. She would call them by their first names, and I did too. I thought I was being a bit naughty by doing that, but I liked to push limits. It was a very comfortable environment.

Chapter 4
Tragedy Strikes

The first major tragedy in my young life took place on my fifth birthday. My grandfather bought me a Flash Gordon helium balloon. Flash Gordon was my hero. He was the captain of a spaceship on television and every week he faced new and harrowing adventures, often involving Ming the Merciless, his mortal enemy. The picture on the balloon was an image of Flash peering intensely through the windshield of the spaceship with crew members, Dale Arden and Dr Zarkov, in the background. I held tightly to my balloon, as I walked proudly down Market Street, with my family in tow. Suddenly a gust of wind tugged at the balloon and the string unraveled from my hand and Flash and crew flew away into the big pine tree at the corner of our front yard. I started screaming and my father and Poppy ran and tried to grab the balloon, but it was too high up in the tree. Before anyone could get a ladder to save it, another gust of wind carried it away. I watched forlornly as it sailed into the stratosphere. After a few miserable moments, realizing that it was beyond human efforts to retrieve, I took comfort in the fact that Flash was flying into space and would forever continue his journey until the end of time or the end of space — whichever came first.

My second major tragedy was also TV hero related. Every week, Captain Midnight would send a special coded message to his closest fans. If you had a Captain Midnight Decoder Ring you could decipher the message. Without one you were lost. When I was in the third grade, I wanted the Decoder Ring more than anything else in the world. It cost a quarter plus the inner wax seal of a jar of Ovaltine, a malt and chocolate flavored powder to be stirred into milk. I saved up my allowance money and my mother bought me a jar. I sent the seal and a quarter to 'Capt. Midnight, Box P, Chicago 77, Illinois'. A long three or four weeks later, a small brown package arrived at home with the ring. I was ecstatic. Now I could decode the secret messages. I was one of Captain Midnight's secret correspondents. I proudly wore the ring to school the next day. I took the school bus that day and when I sat down, some big sixth graders saw my ring and asked me to show it to them. Unsuspecting, I slipped it off my finger and gave it to one of them. After a minute or so I asked for it back. "It's my ring now," announced the boy." My tears did nothing to arouse his compassion as his friends laughed at my naiveté. I never drank Ovaltine again.

Even though she was in her eighties when I was born, Nani Nani walked the eight or nine blocks to *shul* (synagogue) every morning for the six o'clock *minyan* (prayer service) until she was so frail, she couldn't leave the house. I remember her praying all day long (I suppose now that she was saying *Tehillim* — Psalms). She was a very holy woman. Although born in Romania in 1865, a time and place with almost no education for girls, she somehow learned to read Hebrew. She was the prayer leader of the women's section — the only woman who knew how to read from the *siddur* (prayer book). And she understood what she read. She read out loud. When she cried, the others in the women's section would cry. She told me that every day there is a lucky moment when *Hashem* (the Lord) answers your prayers. She *davened* (prayed) all day to catch that lucky time. It was well known in the family that as long as she was alive, nothing bad happened to any of her children or their families. I realize now how difficult a life she must have lived. None of her children were religious nor were her grandchildren and great grandchildren. As far as I know she didn't complain. Of course, she wouldn't eat in any one of her children's or grandchildren's homes, because they didn't keep kosher or if they did, she couldn't trust their standards because they weren't *shomer Shabbos* (Sabbath observers). After she died, each family started to fall apart or was stricken by illness or ill tidings. While her children were superstitious and believed in her ability to intervene with G-d on our behalf, no one thought to take the mantle of prayer and *mitzvohs* (commandments) upon themselves.

She died at home in 1957 at age eighty-nine. I was nine years old. Her funeral was quite unusual. It was held in the main sanctuary of Temple Israel. Normally, Jewish funerals are held in funeral homes. I probably have attended hundreds of funerals since that time and never once in a *shul*, with the exception of funerals for *Roshei Yeshivos* (Heads of Yeshivot), which are occasionally held in the main *beis medrash* (study hall) of their yeshiva. Rabbi Solomon Goldfarb remarked that because she was such an extraordinary woman the *shul* wanted to honor her by making the funeral there. There were rows of Rabbis in flowing caftans and round broad brimmed Black hats from Brooklyn who had made the hour's journey to pay homage to a woman who had generously supported their Jewish institutions with the meagre amounts of money she had. But they didn't come because she was a donor. They came because she was a saintly woman — unique and outstanding in her generation. But I suspect she was much more than that. Although I have no proof, I have a strong assumption that just as her prayers to *Hashem* helped protect and bless all of us, she did the same for the Jewish People. And anyone needing a special blessing for a *refuah shelaima* (a complete recovery from a serious illness) or a child to a childless couple or a match for the matchless could ask her to pray for them.

She sang Yiddish songs to me. One in particular that she sang over and over again was '*Nani nani feigaleh*'. That's why I called her Nani Nani. I didn't understand most of the song except for one line: '*Torah iz die beste sechora*' (Torah is the best merchandise in the world). I think that she and that song had a profound effect on my soul.

Me, wearing my dad's jacket with Nani Nani in the car. Circa 1955.

Every Friday night after *shul,* Cantor Caplow, a wonderfully kind and religious man, would come up to Nani Nani's third floor apartment and make *Kiddush* for her. My brother and I would drink the grape juice. Our parents didn't keep Shabbos and we had no Shabbos meal, but that *Kiddush* made Friday nights a special time for me.

Most likely, as a result of Nani Nani's behavior, presence and tutelage (even though I don't recall her ever lecturing to me) and her *davening* and *Tehilim,* I never questioned the existence of G-d. Granted, for many years I was not *halachically* observant, and if I did a *mitzvah* (a commandment) it was only because I wanted to: but when I was finally convinced that *Hashem* spoke to Moshe (Moses) on Mt. Sinai and that the Jews accepted the commandments upon themselves for all future generations, I was on board.

I now realize that she also taught me lessons in *kiruv rechokim* (bringing those far from Judaism, closer). I still have not fully absorbed them, but I know she was right. If you want to influence people to believe the Torah is true, the best way is to learn with them, show them love and caring and behave in an exemplary manner and never tell them what they must do. That's particularly hard when you're trying to be *mekarev* (to bring someone to observance) your own family, but it probably won't work any other way.

One of my earliest memories is of my maternal grandmother — Momma. We were walking down Market Street (I was probably about four or five) and as we passed an empty lot, we saw a seagull with his leg caught in a tin can. He was flapping his wings but couldn't get very far off the ground because of the can. Momma calmly walked over to the bird and removed his foot from the can. She saw that it was bleeding and carried the bird to our house where she promptly bandaged his leg and wound it tightly with adhesive tape. He flew away. I was very impressed with my grandmother's bravery and kindness. I'm sure she'd be happy to know that one of her great granddaughters, Jessica, became a veterinarian. When Long Beach Hospital was built in the fifties, my grandmother became one of its first 'volunteer pink candy stripers'.

Mom with her parents. Circa 1930.

Once, when she wanted to impress upon me the lesson of always thinking about and doing kindness to others, my mother told me that when she lived in the Bronx as a little girl my grandmother would make her birthday party at a local orphanage, so as to share happiness with those less fortunate. While the story was a demonstration of an altruistic behavior that I never thought I could duplicate (in part because I wasn't aware of any orphanages in Long Beach) the thought was planted in me that my mother was an orphan who was adopted by my grandparents. She was, after all, an only child. By celebrating her birthday at the orphanage, she was going back to her original home. This meant that maybe my mother wasn't Jewish and, therefore, neither was I. This doubt persisted until very recently (2019) when my brother had his DNA tested. The results showed that he was one hundred percent Eastern European Jewish. I breathed a sigh of relief.

Mom with her parents. 1960.

I had a fatalistic view of the world. I don't know when it started. I was born in 1947, soon after the Second World War, and that war and the Holocaust were very vivid memories to those in my parents' and grandparents' generations. I had a very active imagination, and those horrors were very real to me, as well. I often envisioned myself suffering in the death camps. My father and his friends, all Jews, had been soldiers fighting the Nazis in Europe. We had refugees living on our block — people with heavy European accents who had fled from Europe before, during or after the War. Since my sense of time and history was undeveloped, it seemed to me, on one hand, that the Nazis were still ruling Germany and were our mortal enemies, and on the other, that we had defeated them, but only after they killed six million Jews. But even though defeated, they were still lurking around the corner or in alleyways — waiting for their chance to pounce and catch us, take us back to Nazi Germany and shove us into the ovens.

Long Beach, as its eponymous name suggests, is a barrier island or sandbar a few hundred feet off the South Shore of Long Island. There were concrete bunkers spaced every few hundred feet along the beach. They were to provide protection to the machine gunners in case of a naval invasion by the Nazis. No one was manning the bunkers, but I thought they still might be needed to ward off a future attack.

I remember, as an eight-year-old, not wanting laughing gas from the dentist to ease the pain caused by the slow drills. If my relatives had suffered such horrible pain and death by the hands of their Nazi torturers, the least I could do was take a little pain from my nice Jewish dentist who was only trying to fix my cavity. It wasn't very logical, but the emotion was true enough.

My mother encouraged me to eat all the food on my plate so that I could maintain my status as a member in good standing of the 'Clean Plate Club'. This was important, she explained, because, "Think of all the starving children in Europe. If they had this food in front of them, do you know how happy they'd be?" Yes. I wanted to be a member of this club. (When I met my Spanish wife, I told her that she was the reason that I always finished all the food on my plate). My younger brother said: "Why don't you send my food to them?" He obviously didn't 'get it'.

Although I hadn't heard of it yet, 'survival of the fittest' is certainly a truth among humans as well as animals. As a young boy, I was cowardly. I didn't like to fight; didn't like to get hurt; and had a slight stutter. One of the boys on the street, Eddie, was a bully. He used to beat me up almost daily. I would run home to my mother, crying. One day my mother, who was fed up with her sissy son, told me that she didn't want me to be a coward and that I should beat up Eddie so that he wouldn't bully me again. The next time I saw Eddie, I jumped on his back and pounded him with my fists. He ran home crying and I felt vindicated. We became good friends after that.

Another incident proved that 'survival of the fittest' for humans didn't only mean being able to beat up your rival or neighbor but being able to use the governmental systems to your advantage. I was playing marbles with my next-door neighbor, Jerry. I don't remember the catalyst, it probably was because he had lost his 'cat's eye' marble to me, but he got mad and punched me in the face. I think I told him that I was going to call the police. He dared me to do it. I ran home and called the police. "Jerry hit me in the eye," I told the dispatcher. I was crying and she probably couldn't understand me well, but I gave her Jerry's address. About ten minutes later, three police cars, with the sirens screaming, pulled up to Jerry's house. The whole neighborhood was out on the street and on their porches to see what was going on. I told the lead policeman that I was the one who called, and the culprit was inside the house. Five policemen, guns drawn, entered Jerry's house. He and his eight-year-old sister were inside. The cops came out soon afterwards with their pistols holstered and drove away. The lesson was — don't think I won't take you up on a dare.

I learned not to play practical jokes on others from Joe

Palooka. Joe was a professional heavyweight boxer in a popular syndicated cartoon strip. He was sort of a cross between a heavyweight champ and a social worker. One of the networks decided that it would make a popular TV series. I watched a number of episodes. One in particular affected me deeply. It was Thanksgiving. Joe had a friend who was down and out. He had lost his job and he and his family had nothing to eat. This was in the days before food stamps or welfare. Kind hearted Joe stepped in. He went to the grocery store and bought a big twenty-five-pound turkey with all the fixings to bring to his friend's family. The family was deeply depressed when Joe showed up. They were bemoaning their fate. They had nothing to eat that Thanksgiving. Joe knocks on the door. His friend answers it.

"Joe, nice to see you. I'd love to invite you in for a Thanksgiving dinner, but I'm sorry, I don't have anything to offer you.

Joe smiles and says, "Don't worry. I brought you a turkey with all the fixings."

"Joe," says his friend, "you shouldn't have. That's much too much."

"I couldn't let you and your wife and little Billy, and Jeannie go hungry on Thanksgiving. Joe unwraps the turkey from its brown paper wrapping and sets it in the middle of the dining room table. The family is so happy. They haven't eaten for days. They invite Joe to join them. The wife sets the table with their best dishes and silverware, and they sit down. The father says grace. "Thank you, Lord, for this wonderful gift. We're so happy to be Americans celebrating this great holiday."

He takes the large meat fork and the carving knife and jabs

the turkey with the fork.

'Boing'. The fork glances off the turkey. He tries again. The bird is impervious to the fork. The father realizes the turkey is rubber.

"Joe", he says, "tell me it isn't true. Joe, a rubber turkey? Joe, how could you do this to us? Joe. Joe."

Joe has no idea that another friend of his, who was in the car with him after he bought the turkey, thought to play a practical joke on Joe and switched his rubber turkey with Joe's real one.

Joe stumbles out of the house, crestfallen, and in total confusion. He immediately goes back to the grocery store and buys an even larger turkey and then returns to the poor family who welcomes him now with caution but with open arms.

The next day Joe found out what happened, and I learned a lesson that I would never forget. Not that I never played a practical joke on anyone. I did. Many times — but never with a rubber turkey.

I don't know whether it's true for everyone, but for me, growing up next to the Atlantic Ocean profoundly influenced my connection with it. It was also a source of my superpowers. I used to go to the beach almost every day — summer and winter. In the summer I swam, made mud castles on the shore, and dug halfway to China. In the winter I would walk on the boardwalk above the beach and watch the Polar Bear Club members going in for their daily dip. One summer's day, when I was six or seven, I was playing in the water and a great wave swept over my head. Instead of panicking I stood there on the seafloor and saw the top of the wave passing over my head. I don't remember holding my breath and when the wave passed, I calmly walked out of the water onto the beach. Right then I realized that I could breathe underwater. I don't remember when I lost this superpower, but by the time I was seven or eight, I couldn't do it any more.

Another superpower was my ability to see great distances. While I only imagined what China would look like when I finally broke through the Chinese sky with my little shovel, I actually saw the windmills and people skating on the ice beyond the dike in Holland on the other side of the ocean — even though it was summer! My extraordinary vision lasted until junior high school when I couldn't see the writing on the blackboard from my seat in the back of the classroom and was diagnosed with near-sightedness.

From the foregoing you might think I led a sheltered childhood. I did not. My parents exposed me to a world outside of our suburban one in Long Beach. They sometimes took me on a Sunday to Washington Square Park in Manhattan. There I met a different species of human — Beatniks. Beatnik artists displayed their paintings in the Square and other Beatniks played the guitar and sang. They looked very different from the people I grew up with. The men had long, unkempt beards and flannel shirts and dungarees. I remember one of them strumming his guitar and singing:

"Oh, Mr Block, you were born in a lake.
You take the cake.... You take the cake.
Oh, Mr Block you were born in a lake
You take the cake.... You take the cake."

As inane as the lyrics were, the song obviously made a big impression on me. I can hear it now.

We moved a few miles away to Rockville Centre when I was ten. Our neighbor who lived across the street from us,

Larry White, told us a story about a concert he attended at Carnegie Hall. He was sitting next to a Beatnik. Before the concert started, they exchanged pleasantries. The Beatnik asked him: "Where are you from man?"

Larry replied: "Hicksville," (which is where he and his wife were living at the time).

The Beatnik responded, "I know you're from Hicksville man, but where are you from?"

Chapter 5
A Guiding Philosophy

I liked my dentist, Dr Hornstein. His daughter, Brooke, was in my class at school. I liked him so much that I decided that when I grew up, I'd be a dentist. When I announced this to my parents, at the age of seven or eight, my mother said, "And look into people's dirty mouths all day?" That was enough for me. I had no trouble picturing myself as a dentist having to look into dirty mouths filled with rotting teeth and horribly smelling breath. I was not going to be a dentist.

This odd exchange with my mother was, in a way, typical of her manner of guiding me. Although it sounds ridiculous to me now, to tell a seven- or-eight-year-old what his profession should or should not be, in those days it was common. Among Jewish families, boys were encouraged to become doctors or lawyers and girls, teachers. Like my mother, who was a pianist, I had long, slim fingers and even as a young boy, could stretch my hands over an octave, which were ideal for playing that instrument. My aunts used to remark, whenever they saw me play, "Oh look at those fingers. He should be a surgeon." Neither my mother or father, however, ever told me what career or profession they wanted me to pursue. My mother used to say: "I don't care if you're a garbage man, as long as you're happy." A garbage man was OK, but not a dentist.

To the outside world I probably seemed like an average kid. I did passably well in elementary school but was not an outstanding student or athlete or musician. There is a comfort in being average. Not much is expected of you. You could fail or come short without fear of embarrassment or punishment. But in truth, I knew that I was not an average kid. I had ideas, talents and powers that I didn't discuss with anyone, but which I recognized as unusual. I could hit a small target with a paperclip shot from a rubber band at ten paces — without aiming. I practiced this relentlessly — stepping off ten paces and suddenly whirling around and shooting the paperclip into the center of the cardboard target. On my eighth birthday Poppy took me to Ringling Brothers Barnum and Bailey Circus in Madison Square Garden. We saw sword swallowers and the tallest man in the world, but the most fascinating attraction for me was the knife thrower. A woman was strapped, spread eagle, to a plywood disc which was then spun at increasing speed while the knife thrower threw his knives at the spinning woman until they outlined her body. I resolved to master this feat. With money saved up from many weeks of allowance, I bought a throwing knife at Hoffritz, a paradisiacal emporium of sharp objects. I practiced for hours every day throwing the knife at a cardboard target. Had there been an Olympic event in paperclip shooting, I was convinced that I was gold medal material, although I wasn't so sure that I could beat Ringling's knife thrower in the knife-throwing Olympic event.

Morty was my best friend in elementary school. He was a fair-haired boy and the best boy student in our class. It's possible that some of the girls might have been better students, but, at the age of eight or nine, I was chauvinistic and believed in the inherent superiority of boys — with one exception. A girl in the class had cerebral palsy and couldn't write very legibly, but she was very bright and the class's best math student. I was fortunate to have her in my class, as I learnt an important lesson about disabilities at a very young age. They have nothing to do with intelligence.

Morty and I were close friends even after we moved about six miles away to another town, Rockville Centre, where my father had his dress shop. I was ten. After we moved, I once spent a Shabbos in Morty's house. It was an experience that I'll never forget. Although my great-grandmother lived with us and was a very religious woman, I couldn't relate to her in the way I related to my best friend.

My favorite TV show in those years was *The Twilight Zone*. It aired at nine p.m. on Friday night. It never occurred to me that keeping Shabbos meant that one couldn't watch *The Twilight Zone*. When I went to Morty's house for Shabbos, I noticed that all the light switches were covered. He explained that it was forbidden to turn on or off lights on Shabbos. I thought I would miss *Twilight Zone*. Shortly before nine p.m. as we were going to bed in Morty's room, the TV turned on automatically and *The Twilight Zone* came on the screen. After the show was over, the TV turned itself off. I thought my friend was the most religious kid in the world.

Chapter 6
My Father's Family

Growing up in the late fifties and early sixties, my family was not like those I saw on TV. Our house was not like Ricky and Lucy Ricardo's. My mother was a musician and a musical theatre performer, but not daft like Lucy. My father was a solid American and not given to bouts of rage like Cuban Ricky. There was no Fred and Ethel in our lives — no old vaudevillians, now retired, but up for a part in Lucy's crazy antics. It wasn't a family like 'Leave it to Beaver'. I was the older brother, but nothing like the responsible and protective Wally, although my brother did show a certain physical resemblance to the Beaver. My parents were nothing like Ward and June Cleaver. They were the Protestant family that lived in another part of America. Ours certainly wasn't like Ozzie and Harriet's home. Life was difficult. Money was tight. My father had a small women's dress store. My mother was a part time piano teacher. They eked out a living. Fortunately for us, my mother's parents were fairly well off and helped us out so that we could live a comfortable middle-class life.

My family was somewhat different to most Jewish families we knew. My father was not a New Yorker. He came from a small town in Southwestern Pennsylvania — Mount Pleasant — not far from the West Virginia border. In the early 1900s, when my grandparents settled there, it was the place where *landsmen* from his old *shtetl* in Lithuania had started a Jewish community in the New World. It had about seventy Jewish families and a large *shul* with a *rov* (rabbi) and a *cheder* (religious school). The *shochet/melamed* (ritual slaughterer/teacher) would come to town once a week from Pittsburgh (about forty-five miles northeast) and *shecht* (slaughter) the cows and chickens and teach the children. There were many little towns like Mount Pleasant scattered all over the Northeast and the Midwest, with their little Jewish communities established by *landschaften* from the little *shtetls* in Europe. Interestingly enough it also had a sizable 'Syrian' community who also settled there at the same time as the Litvaks. These 'Syrians' were Christians and like the Jews, were merchants. In the late 1800s and early 1900s the Ottoman Empire called the region now comprising Syria, Lebanon, Jordan and Israel — 'Syria'. These two groups owned almost all the retail stores in town.

Mount Pleasant is in coal country, and because of the coal fires on slag heaps that had been burning for over one hundred years, the air smelled of rotten eggs. My father's parents weren't travelers. They never visited New York during my lifetime. We would drive down to Mount Pleasant once every couple of years for Rosh Hashana. I enjoyed the trip. We took Route 76, the Pennsylvania Turnpike. It cut through the deep woods (from which Pennsylvania derives its name — Penn's Wood, as in England's prime minister, William Penn) and tunneled through mountains. My father remembered when it was built in the thirties. According to him, many men died as they blasted and dug the many long and dark tunnels through the Appalachian Mountains. As the turnpike passed into coal country the pervasive smell of rotten eggs from the sulfurous Bituminous coal deposits and slag heap fires made me cringe. Although, after spending a couple of days in Mount Pleasant, I got used to it. I associated the coal dust dinginess of the place with its run-down homes and buildings and the smell of the sulfur with my grandparents' native land. My grandfather was from a small *shtetl* near Minsk and my grandmother from a small town in the province of Vilna. This was Lithuania or greater Poland at the time they were born. I never had any desire to visit Eastern Europe, perhaps because I felt that having been in Mount Pleasant, I had already seen what it looked like and there was no point in 'revisiting' such a depressing place.

My grandparents spoke Yiddish. My grandmother wasn't fluent in English, and I had a hard time understanding her. My grandfather was more fluent in English but wasn't a big talker. When I knew him, my grandfather was a farmer. He had a couple of acres behind the house with a huge, rotting barn filled with rusting farming equipment. He grew tomatoes, cucumbers and peppers. He didn't always do that. During the Depression he raised cattle. Or to be more precise, he would buy a steer and fatten it up and sell it to the kosher butcher. He apparently never could afford more than one steer at a time. Before that, according to my father, he had the largest furniture business in Western Pennsylvania. He was a millionaire, at least on paper. After the stock market crash of 1929, he lost just about everything except his house — a tiny three-bedroom, barely big enough for a family of six children.

My father was a renowned athlete in Mount Pleasant. He was a star running-back on the football team at Ramsey High. He also excelled at basketball and baseball. When he graduated high school, he was offered an athletic scholarship at a small college in Ohio. But it was the Depression and he needed to work and contribute to the family. He worked as a bookkeeper for the Pennsylvania Liquor Control Board. And then came the war. On December 7, 1941, the day of the attack on Pearl Harbor, my father was twenty-one. He was among the first to receive a draft notice.

My father kept his uniform (he was a First Sergeant by the end of the war) in a closet at the back of his dress shop and would put it on periodically. I loved to see him in it, although by the time I was a small boy, the uniform was pulling at the buttons. He also had a bayonet that he said he took from a dead Italian soldier. He trained as a medic and was first assigned to Walter Reed Hospital in Washington, DC.

My dad in Italy. 1944.

He told me that during his first few months, he took care of General Pershing, the senior American general of the First World War who was quite old and sick. He later shipped overseas with Patton's Fifth Army and served as a medic and quartermaster in North Africa and Italy. Fortunately for me, he was unharmed, although he told me that he almost died from something called 'Q' fever — the 'Q' standing for 'query'. My father was working in a field hospital in Algeria where, it seems, that the Army was investigating a strain of a certain virus for use as a biological weapon. Somehow the virus escaped from a test tube and infected many of the hospital staff. The doctors had no idea how to treat it. Many died. My father was in a coma for over a week and then fully recovered.

In early 1945, after Germany had surrendered, the Army offered him a promotion to Second Lieutenant and a trip to the Far East to fight Japan if he re-enlisted. He didn't and returned to the States at the end of the war.

His sister, Frieda, had married Al Glock, whose family had settled in the North Country of New York at the beginning of the twentieth century. They lived in Ogdensburg, at the intersection of the Oswegatchie River and the St. Lawrence River — just across the Ogdensburg—Prescott International Bridge from Johnstown, Ontario. Freida invited Dad to come and stay with them for a while. He did, and after a couple of weeks and with no other plans, began helping Al at his boys' and men's clothing store. In the summer of 1946, Clara and Nate Abel invited their niece, Elinor, a sophomore at New Paltz Teacher's College, to come up to Ogdensburg for the summer. The families made the suggestion and the two went out on a date one evening. My mother told me that she found it funny that my dad wore sunglasses on their evening date, but she didn't say anything. She thought he was trying to look cool. In truth he didn't want her to know that he was near-sighted. Although he was nine years older than Elinor, the age difference didn't bother either of them. They got married at my grandparent's house in Long Beach in November 1946.

My parents at their wedding reception. 1946.

Dad's older brother, Uncle Sam, was an accountant for the State of Pennsylvania for most of his working life. He was also in the Army during the War, but he was Stateside, working as an accountant. A number of the Semenow sisters went to Washington DC during the war to work for the government. Two of them settled there. Aunt Margie married Roland Hartman, who became a prosperous businessman in the DC area. He was in the food supply business. His son, Daniel, eventually took over the business. They also had a daughter, Irene, who's married to a partner in a large DC law firm.

Dad's sister, Aunt Betty stayed in the Washington area after the war and worked for years at the CIA. According to family lore, she typed up transcriptions of wiretaps on Russians in Washington. She suspected that she was being followed wherever she went. Although she voiced concerns to her superiors, they told her that she was imagining it. She eventually had a nervous breakdown and retired on a full pension. Aunt Betty never married. Years later, I read in the papers that the CIA actually did surveillance on their employees. But that was too late to help Aunt Betty.

My dad's other sister, Belle, married Marty Levitt from Messena, NY, a city about sixty miles east of Ogdensburg, also on the St. Lawrence River. Messena is famous for being the location of a large Alcoa Aluminum plant. Uncle Marty had a furniture store there. They couldn't have children and adopted a girl from a local Indian Reservation — my cousin Judy. In researching the history of Massena on Wikipedia, I came across the following interesting item — which I had never heard of before.

The Messina Blood Libel

The Massena blood libel was an instance of blood libel against Jews in which the Jews of Massena, New York, were falsely accused of the kidnapping and ritual murder of a Christian girl in September 1928.

On September 22nd, 1928, two days before Yom Kippur, four-year-old Barbara Griffiths went for a walk and did not come back home. After a long search by townspeople and state police, a rumor began to circulate that the girl had been kidnapped and killed by the town's Jews for a religious ritual associated with the impending holiday.

The following day, the state police questioned Morris Goldberg, a Jew with little knowledge of Jewish tradition. Goldberg left police with the impression that there might be some truth to the rumors that Jews engaged in ritual murder.

At that point, the state police sought to interrogate Rabbi Berel Brennglass, leader of the town's Adath Israel synagogue. When asked about the allegations of ritual murder, Brennglass told the police and the town's mayor, who was present, that they should be ashamed for asking such questions. He expressed outrage that people believed such lies in the United States in the twentieth century.

Barbara Griffiths was found in the woods later that afternoon roughly a mile from her home. She told authorities she had become lost during her walk and slept in the forest. Nevertheless, some citizens of Massena continued to believe that Griffiths had been kidnapped by the Jews. They attributed her safe return to the discovery of the Jew's plot.

The Massena blood libel drew national attention.

> Through the efforts of Rabbi Brennglass, the American Jewish Committee and the American Jewish Congress denounced the town's leaders, prompting apologies from the mayor and the state police to the rabbi, the town's Jews, and all Jews of the United States. In his apology, the mayor wrote:

"In light of the solemn protest of my Jewish neighbors, I feel I ought to express clearly and unequivocally ... my sincere regret that by any act of commission or omission, I should have seemed to lend countenance ... to what I should have known to be a cruel libel imputing human sacrifice as a practice now or at any time in the history of the Jewish people."

Feldberg, Michael (ed.) (2002). "The Massena Blood Libel". *Blessings of Freedom: Chapters in American Jewish History*. New York: American Jewish Historical Society. ISBN 0-88125-756-7. Archived from the original on September 17, 2010. Retrieved December 3, 2008.

Geography and history were my favorite subjects in school. I loved learning the names and order of the presidents and, of course, we had to memorize the states and their capitals. Wherever I went I paid close attention to the physical layout of the place. Later, when I worked for Pioneer Title Company, my favorite activity was drawing maps of the title I was researching.

I remember well my first trip to Ogdensburg by train. I was probably about seven or eight years old. It was summer. We took the NY Central and slept in a Pullman car. I was so excited to be on the train and to see scenery that I could barely sleep. We stayed with my aunt Clara. A swift river ran down the middle of town — the Oswegatchie. I loved that name. Both Uncle Al and Uncle Nate had 'camps' — vacation cabins

— on the St. Lawrence. One early morning we motored over to the Abel's camp and went out fishing on their boat. The St. Lawrence is quite wide in Ogdensburg and the river is dotted with the 'Thousand Islands'. Many people have heard of Thousand Island dressing, but probably don't know where its name comes from. The Thousand Islands are like sparkling green gems in the blue of the river. There are well over one thousand islands. Some of the islands have a single mansion or castle. It was a very popular vacation destination for the rich in the late nineteenth and early twentieth centuries.

Aunt Clara had packed a lunch for us 'fishermen'. I don't recall catching any fish, but the sandwich was the best sandwich I ever had in my life. It was sardines with onions on toasted rye with mayonnaise. In the subsequent many years, I often make that sandwich — I really like it, but it doesn't come close to the taste of the sandwich that early morning on the St. Lawrence with the summer sun warming us gently and the slow breeze of the cool river air. For me that was 'the sandwich'. Years later, when I was in Paris with my daughter Yochi, I was reminded of that day. On my way back to our hotel from *shul,* I bought some fresh *baguettes* and Camembert cheese from the kosher bakery for our breakfast. Yochi told me that it was the best sandwich she ever had in her life. I knew the feeling.

Chapter 7
My Mother's Family

My maternal grandparents.
Circa 1960.

My mother's family was from New York City. My maternal great-grandfather, Solomon Siegel, for whom I'm named, came to America in the middle 1890s and settled in the Lower East Side. After working for about a year, he sent for my great-grandmother and the children. In a tape that she made shortly before she died (in the early 1980s), my great-aunt, Ernestine (my grandmother's sister) recounted the family's coming to America in August 1896. They left their home in Bucharest and traveled by train to Hamburg, Germany for the trip across the ocean on the Hamburg American Line ship *Phoenicia*. My aunt was five years old, and my grandmother was one and a half, their sister Charlotte was three and the oldest, Michael, was seven. The two youngest sisters, Sadie and Clara were born in New York.

Ernestine was heartbroken at having to leave her maternal grandmother and her great-grandmother. In fact, her grandmother, Rosa Furman, had planned to travel with them on the boat, but her husband, who (believe it not) was in the fur business, refused. He was apparently quite successful and wanted to move his family closer to his source of furs — Siberia! A few years later, in 1899, after getting a divorce from her husband (the reason given was because no one in their right mind would willingly move to Siberia), Rosa came to America and moved in with her children in the Bronx. She died in 1915 and was buried in the Baron Hirsch Cemetery on Staten Island.

Ernestine remembers the monotony of the trip (she made it sound like it took a few months to cross while it only took twelve days) in 'storage' — the lowest class, and that her mother was sick in bed almost the whole trip over. They shared a tiny cabin with one of their cousins and her family. The only kosher food they were served was hard black bread and herring. Their cousin had a large hamper of cookies in the cabin and my aunt would steal cookies from the hamper with regularity. When they got to America, they stayed with other cousins on the Lower East Side and my aunt describes seeing and tasting the most exotic fruit that she ever laid eyes on — a banana. They arrived in August and school started that fall. Everything was so different from what she had known up to then. Even the Romanian Yiddish that they spoke was different from the Lithuanian Yiddish that was the *lingua franca* of the Jews on the Lower East Side. She and my great grandmother were constantly misunderstanding the local denizens and *vice versa*. One conversation that stuck in her memory was a Jewish mother who recounted to another that her son "*er gefaln fun di fenster aun iz geven gehrget".* (He fell from the window and was *"gehrget"*)" In my aunt's Yiddish *"gehrget"* meant that he was killed. Yet the woman didn't seem overly distraught. My great grandmother told her that to a *Litvak* 'gehrget' also meant 'hurt' and also that she knew the storyteller lived on the ground floor of the tenement, so the injury must have been quite minor.

My great grandfather, according to family history, was by this time a 'Yiddish poet' which I understood to mean that he didn't work and most likely didn't earn a living. I am not aware of anything that he published. My mother said that she never saw him without a *sefer (holy book)* in his hands. He was always learning *Torah*. My great grandmother took on the burden of supporting the family and sold candy from

My maternal grandfather. Circa 1925

the apartment, eventually opening up a small candy store. In my great grandmother's living room in Long Beach there was a small, framed photograph of the man whom I believed to be my namesake. He was a smart looking man with a bushy moustache and a big tan fedora, crouching behind a rock. I was told that this was a photograph of my great grandfather when he was a scout for Teddy Roosevelt in Cuba during the Spanish American War of 1897. Years later I learned that someone in the family had clipped out a picture of a man who was indeed a scout for Teddy Roosevelt and looked somewhat like my great-grandfather and framed it. But he hadn't been in that war.

Aunt Ernestine described her bewildering first day of school. She had little understanding of English, and the customs of American schools and American children were very foreign to her. On her way home that day, her crinoline fell onto the sidewalk. She froze in her tracks and cried until a kindly older girl took her hand and brought her home. Though reluctant and embarrassed to go to school the next day, she returned. And she persisted.

By the time she finished eighth grade, she was the valedictorian of her class. But in the early aughts of the twentieth century, most girls from working class homes did not go to high school but started working. She worked as a secretary in a plumbing supply business on the Upper East Side of New York. She was elegant and well mannered. Her sister, my grandmother, worked as a secretary for the Studebaker car company at their New York headquarters until she married. My sister, Deena Rochel, has a large set of beautiful 24-carat, gold-rimmed glassware that the company gave my grandmother as a wedding present in the early 1920s.

Ernestine describes her outings to Sacandaga Park in the Adirondack Mountains in the teens and early 20s on Sundays in the summer. She would take the New York Central from the city to Schenectady and then transfer to the Fonda Johnstown and Gloversville Railroad. The trip was four to five hours each way. She loved to sit on the lawn outside the Adirondack Inn, which was owned by the Railroad and listen to the band concerts. Jews were not allowed inside the hotel and although I have no idea how anyone could have known she was Jewish, she accepted the segregationist rules and never entered. It was her dream to get away from the dirt and grime of the city. She and her husband later bought a home in Sacandaga Lake Park, which eventually became a summer community for many Jews living in the Amsterdam and Gloversville area. By the time my parents bought a home there, even the Sacandaga Lake Country Club allowed Jewish members (something that the Rockville Links — in our hometown, did not).

Ernestine married Arthur Leventhal, who had graduated from NYU and its law school a few years before America entered the First World War. Her sister, Sadie, married Arthur's good friend from college, Nathan Goodman, who graduated at about the same time with a degree in civil engineering. Arthur practiced law for a few years, but by the time I was born, in 1947, he was the president and owner of Frank Brothers Shoes — a high-end shoe manufacturer and retailer in New York. He was quite successful. My mother told me that when she got engaged to my father, soon after WWII, my Uncle Arthur hosted an engagement party for them at the Russian Tea Room on 57th St. in Manhattan and threw twenty-dollar bills onto the stage for the dancing Cossacks to spear with their daggers. That's when twenty dollars was a week's salary for a factory worker. They lived in a beautiful eight-room apartment on the Upper East Side and my aunt had a magnificent loft for her painting studio on 57th Street. They were Jewish NY intellectuals and their circle of friends included musicians, artists, writers, lawyers and judges. My mother was fond of attending her parties, whenever she was invited. My aunt was, in a way, a kind of *entre* to a world much different than ours, and one that my mother aspired to.

My grandmother and at least two of her sisters were quite

good amateur artists. Aunt Ernestine was probably the best painter of the three. She took lessons from famous artists in New York and spent most of her days painting. She won a prize for the best still life from the Art Students League of New York in the fifties. We have the painting in our living room. My grandmother also took up painting and was quite good at it. We also have a still life with fruits of hers hanging in our house. Aunt Sadie was a sculptress. My grandmother told me that as a teen she had won first prize for the best soap sculpture in New York City. I never saw any of her work, but her daughter, my cousin Marjorie Goodman, is an incredible artist. She studied art in college and although her day job was as a social worker for Suffolk County, her main activity was her art. Her early works are beautiful paintings of ballet dancers and portraits of people. Later in life she experimented with light and her paintings were abstract and many were white on white. According to my brother, who is quite artistic in his own right, the world has never seen paintings as beautiful as her white-on-white paintings. Like my Aunt Ernestine, while she exhibited her paintings, she would never agree to sell one, and gave away only very few to family and friends.

Uncle Arthur had a niece, Rhonda, who was married to a wealthy real estate developer, the builder of large cookie-cutter housing developments for returning servicemen on Long Island and Pennsylvania. My mother and I visited them when I was about eight or nine at their estate in Westchester. They lived in what can only be described as a feudal castle. One drove through the gates of the estate on a road with modest brick houses on both sides. These were for the servants, groundskeepers and other staff. It was an enormous estate with many acres and its own golf course. (Cousin Rhonda was a championship golfer). They had a son, a few years older than me, James, who had a few rooms in the house, one of which was filled floor to ceiling with toys, model ships and planes, and games still in their unopened boxes. It was surreal. James was dressed in an authentic Superman outfit — cape and all. We ran around the woods on the estate for a while and then played with his extensive train set — like something out of a Christmas display at Macy's. His parents divorced and Rhonda married the Chief Justice of the Supreme Court of New Jersey. When I was in high school, I got to meet him. He was a graduate of Cornell and indicated to my parents that he would try to use his influence to get me in. In the end I didn't apply there.

As you might surmise, my mother was a bit of a social climber. When I was in first grade, she started taking diction lessons. I remember one phrase that she repeated over and over again: "I'm picking up paw paws and putting them in my pocket." I have no idea why this sentence should have made her sound like a high-falutin' lady and not like some Jewish princess from the Bronx now living in Long Beach, but I'm sure the teacher knew what he was teaching. My little brother and I used to mimic her. She was very elegant and enjoyed dressing up and hosting or going to dinner parties, the latest Broadway shows, and the opera. We had a first-tier center box at Carnegie Hall for the NY Philharmonic's season every year. She called it the 'Royal Box' because that's where Queen Elizabeth with Prince Phillip and their entourage would sit in London's concert hall. I suppose I felt this class thing too and despite my egalitarian nature, aspired to be part of a higher class.

My Aunt Ernestine's son, Melvin, my mother's first cousin, was an Air Force pilot. When WWII broke out, Uncle Arthur used his influence and got him into the Army Air Corps even though he was only seventeen. He rose in rank and eventually became a full Colonel and Wing Commander. He flew many missions over the 'Hump' in Burma during the Second World War and again in Korea and then in Vietnam. When I was about eight or nine, he taught me how to defend myself if attacked by a North Korean soldier wielding a knife. I should block the downward thrust of his knife by grabbing the inside of his right arm with my hand above his elbow while extending my right foot over his right foot so as to catch him off balance and throw him to the ground. Then I should stab him in the neck with my own knife. In my mind I didn't think this move was that practical, because I was a little kid, and the North Korean was a big strong man. I thought I would be better off throwing my knife at him (like Jim Bowie in the Alamo). Fortunately, I've never had to do either.

My mother's Aunt Clara was married to a man from the 'North Country', Nate Abel. Nate had an auto parts store in Ogdensburg, NY. They had a son, Richard, who served time in prison for manslaughter. He was in the Merchant Marine at the time (sometime in the fifties) and killed a fellow sailor in a drunken brawl. After he was released, he became a traveling salesman and would come to our house every now and then and try to sell my parents something he was hawking.

Aunt Sadie, as I said earlier, was married to Nat Goodman. Nat was a civil engineer and family legend has it that he was one of the main engineers on the Queens-Midtown tunnel. During the war, the Army assigned a car and driver to chauffeur him to and from work.

Poppy was born in New York in 1891. He died in 1961. His given name was David. As mentioned earlier, he was a Cohen. He grew up in the Bronx and was a die-hard Yankee fan. He had great hopes that I would become a Yankee player and the home run king of 1969. He died before he could see that his dream for me was unfulfilled. I suppose that's some consolation. My second cousin, Rhoda Brookfield, (nee Farenthal), self-published a very well-written slim volume about her mother Jenny's family — the Gladstones. Included in it is the story of how her mother met and married my grandfather's brother Nathan. The Gladstones were almost Jewish royalty in the Bronx. The *paterfamilias* who called himself 'Grandpa Jones', went into the shirt making business in the late 1880s with a young *goyishe* shirt maker named Van Heusen. They did quite well, becoming the major shirt manufacturer in the country. The Farenthals, by comparison, were more recent immigrants and not nearly as successful. But they were smart and hardworking and eventually all the brothers did well in business. I don't know anything about Poppy's boyhood. I assumed he graduated from high school, but I don't really know. In 1917, when the US entered the First World War, he was drafted into the US Army and sent to Fort Hood in Texas for training. He had been dating my grandmother and wrote to her daily. Fortunately, the war ended before he shipped out to Europe. On his return to New York, he got a job as a shipping clerk for K and R Dresses — a manufacturer of middle priced dresses — in the Garment District at 1400 Broadway. He eventually worked his way up in the firm and became a senior executive.

The Farenthals were a close-knit family. They vacationed together in Hot Springs, Arkansas and the Caribbean and they invested together. Poppy's brother, Lou, managed the building at 1410 Broadway and had the opportunity to buy into it as a minor partner. He also advised his brothers to invest. That building eventually produced a nice, if modest, income for many family members for many years. We sold it about thirty years ago. They also cared very much for each other. They had an unmarried sister, Dede. She was very sweet, but somewhat homely and unsuccessful in finding a husband. She was probably in her early thirties when her brothers concocted a plan to get her married. They found an unmarried Jewish merchant marine sailor — Fred — who was short and funny looking, but a really outgoing and nice guy and offered him $5000 and a job as an elevator operator in their building to marry their sister. Dede found her husband. Of course, they never breathed a word of their plot to her.

Poppy was very civic minded and when he moved to Long Beach, he became aware of the corruption in the city. It wasn't too hard to figure out. There were traffic lights on the corner of every street. I don't recall any stop signs. This was quite unusual for such a small city. People said that the Mafia forced the city to buy traffic lights from one of their gang members. Poppy had a letter published in the New York Times in 1936 drawing attention to the corruption in the City of Long Beach. Fortunately for us, no action was taken by the mob against my grandfather-crusader. In the movie, 'The Godfather', the home of the Corleone Family was Long Beach. In fact, it was the home of the Luchesse family. People used to say that it was good that they were based there, because they wouldn't tolerate any crime in their own hometown (that wasn't done by them). Long Beach was a quiet city.

I was very close to Poppy. When I was on vacation from school, he would take me to work with him. We took the Long Island Railroad from Long Beach to Penn Station and then walked the few blocks to his office. The best part of the train ride, which took about an hour, was when it would cross Reynold's Channel — separating Long Beach from Island Park and the rest of Long Island. The trestle was just wide enough for the train and there were no walls around it to obstruct the view. It was as if the train was just floating on top of the water.

After arriving in NYC, we would stop off at a Horn and Hardart's for some hot chocolate and a slice of apple pie. The restaurant fascinated me. Near the door was a booth where a cashier made change and dispensed nickels. The food was behind small windows in the walls of the place — sandwiches of all kinds; pies and cakes; drinks; fruits, etc. To access the food, you inserted the required number of nickels into the slot next to your selection, the little glass door would unlock, and you took your food. Hands on the other side of the wall would quickly replace your item. Coffee, tea and hot chocolate were dispensed through the mouths of brass lions — aligned along the bottom of the food wall.

At Poppy's work, I got lots of pencils embossed with the letters K and R. In the mid-fifties, his boss had a remote-control TV installed in the office. I had heard of color TVs, although it would be many years until we owned one, but I hadn't even heard of remote control. Granted, it wasn't like any remote control that became commercially available later, it was more like the knob for changing channels had been pulled out of the television casing and mounted on a box a few feet away. But it meant you didn't have to get out of your chair to change channels. Now that was progress!

My mother was a gifted pianist. She took lessons as a young girl and continued until her marriage. She played and was a soloist with the Long Beach High School Orchestra. The music director of the school was Glen Glenn, a xylophonist for Xavier Cugat's Orchestra. (Glenn had a music camp that I later attended as a teen). She could play anything. When I started taking piano lessons, I could only marvel at her playing even more. She could take a very difficult piece of music that she had never seen before and sight-read it flawlessly. The more I learned the more astounded I was. I have no idea how she (or anyone, for that matter) could take a Chopin Polonaise or a Beethoven Sonata or the Bumble Bee Boogie and sight-read the music, which was black with notes and played at lightning speed with both hands, at first reading.

As a young child I assumed that Liberace was the greatest pianist in the world. The reason was simple. He had a TV show, and no other pianist did. His piano was a nine-foot concert grand with crystal candelabras, and he played really fast. However, I had this heretical idea that the universe (or the Networks — which were virtually the same) had messed up. In my opinion my mother was at least as good and maybe better. She should have been on television instead of Liberace.

And she was a performer. She was very active in Hadassah, eventually becoming a Life President. The highlight of the local organization's year was a musical production. My mother would write all the lyrics (usually adopting the music from hit Broadway shows) and would, of course, star as a singer and dancer, when not accompanying others on the piano.

Her love of Broadway musicals was consuming. My parents had a collection of records that included every musical ever recorded on Broadway, along with an extensive collection of classical music. The record player was always on when she was home, and she was constantly singing along with the show tunes. She also had what I grew to consider an annoying habit of answering every question by singing an appropriate line from a musical. Needless to say, she knew every line in every show by heart. That feat did not impress me nearly as much as her piano playing, but it was still impressive. (However, she has been overshadowed in that regard by my daughter and her granddaughter, Yocheved Raizel, who can sing the lyrics to almost every known song from the thirties until today. Thank G-d *she* doesn't answer questions with lyrics.)

When we moved to Rockville Centre, in 1958, my mother bought a Steinway Grand piano that had been built in Hamburg in 1938. Our family never bought anything made in Germany. It was our way of boycotting the Nazis, who, I was told, were still running many of the major companies there. The one exception that was made was the Steinway. There were a number of factors allowing it to avoid our boycott. 1938 was before the extermination of Jews had begun and when Jews were still allowed to leave Germany; it was purchased second hand from a private person who lived nearby, so no Nazi would benefit from the sale; and it was a bargain that would probably not present itself again in a lifetime. It was a beautiful instrument and my mother loved it and together they proved beyond a doubt that she was better than Liberace. Oh, and she also placed a candelabra on it.

My great grandparents, Solomon and Deena Rochel Siegel with children Michael, Ernestine (with the parasol) Sadie and Bessie. (Taken at Saks 34th St. New York in the 1890s).

My father, Master Sergeant US Army.

CHAPTER 8
Rockville Centre

This is not a typo, nor a faux British pretension. In seventh grade social studies we learnt about the political subdivisions of New York State and the history of our county and village. I still remember the history of my village's name. In the 1840s a local entrepreneur, a Mr Robert Pettit, living in the town of Hempstead, Nassau County, on the south shore of Long Island, applied to the Federal Government to open a US post office in his general store. He needed a name for the location. He decided to honor one of the area's distinguished citizens at the time, the Reverend Mordechai Smith, a miller and pastor of the local Methodist church. He first requested 'Smithtown', but it was already taken by a village in nearby Suffolk County. 'Smithville' was also not a viable alternative for some reason that I don't remember. Undaunted, Mr Petit tried again. The Reverend Smith was of Scottish ancestry and belonged to the 'Rock' clan. Unfortunately, 'Rockville' was taken by a town in Maryland, so he opted for 'Rockville Centre'. The spelling might have been a marketing ploy as the owner of the general store, Mr Pettit, was also a partner in a real estate development firm and 'Centre' looked posher than 'Center'. In ads he ran in various newspapers in Queens, a populous contiguous county (not yet part of the City of New York), he proclaimed: 'Gentlemen seeking a country seat will find it to their advantage to secure lots in said village'. In fact, it soon became a haven for retired whaling captains from Maine — a kind of American maritime aristocracy, I suppose — although there couldn't possibly have been enough whaling captains in the whole eastern seaboard to fill even a medium size village. Fortunately for the developers, the Long Island Railroad opened a station in Rockville Centre in 1867. Now residents could commute to New York City in less than an hour and Rockville Centre became a suburb. It became an incorporated village in 1893.

We moved to Rockville Centre in February of 1958. By that time, the middle-class descendants of Irish and Italian Catholics and Eastern European Jews had eclipsed Mr Pettit's 'gentleman'. I was ten years old and in fifth grade. Although I was four when I started first grade, I had been sick for much of that year with a sore throat and fever. My pediatrician, Dr Pisacano, concluded that the problem was tonsillitis. He recommended a tonsillectomy. In the early fifties this procedure was quite common for young children with sore throats and inflamed tonsils. Tonsils were considered vestigial organs, so why not remove them? (Today, science recognizes that they play an important part in the body's immune system — too late for me.) My parents told me it was no big deal, that I'd be in the hospital for a day or so and the hospital would serve me ice cream to soothe my throat. That didn't sound so bad. I had the procedure done that spring in a local hospital. When the operation was about to begin, I was wheeled into the operating room and a damp rag soaked with ether was held over my mouth and nose. The doctor told me to count down from ten. I got to eight or seven when I saw a swirling vortex, and then the next thing I saw, was my parents standing over me in the recovery room and telling me that everything was fine. I was waiting for the ice cream. I remember feeling cheated when I was given ice chips to soothe the pain. I don't know if my parents deliberately lied to me; or that in their day, ice cream was the preferred palliative after a tonsillectomy and they assumed it still was or perhaps, the hospital ran out of ice cream. Since then, I have been suspicious of any second hand or hearsay testimony. In any case, the procedure worked. My sore throats stopped. My mother decided that since I had missed so much school and was very young, I should be held back. I was unhappy with her decision because I liked my friends in school, but what could I do? In the end, it turned out to be a blessing. Had she let me stay with my class, I would have graduated college at twenty and would have faced Vietnam a year earlier.

With the move, the ethnicity of my friends changed. Whereas Long Beach was a majority Jewish city, Rockville Centre was not. It was, and still is, the seat of the Archbishop of the Catholic Church of Long Island and had a majority population of Catholics. The Catholics went to St. Agnes Catholic School. The only non-Jews in the public schools were a few Protestants and the Catholic kids who were thrown out of St. Agnes for bad behavior. I was drawn to the Protestants. While I had some Jewish friends, my best friends were my neighbors, the brothers Johnny and Bobby Delfaunt. They belonged to the Congregational Church.

As a result of our friendship, I joined their Boy Scout troop which met in the basement of the Congregational Church. I don't know if the reason I liked my troop so much had anything to do with Protestants, but I suspect that it did. It was quite different from the Jewish Boy Scout troop in town which met at the Reform Synagogue. Our family belonged to Temple Beth Shalom, a conservative synagogue, which had no Boy Scout troop. There were days when the boys from the Jewish troop came to school in their uniforms. We never did. They had badges and ranks far above ours. In our troop, it was considered to be bad manners and very much out of place to attain a rank higher than Second Class Scout. We were in the Scouts for the camaraderie and the fun. The Jews, on the other hand, were into achievement badges and high ranks. At least, that's the way it seemed to me. I was, in a way, becoming something of an anti-Semite.

The only First-Class Scout in our troop was the troop leader, who was much older than we were. He was probably in his early twenties. The leader's father was the Village Engineer, Mr Keller, and the family was quite well to do. They owned a vacation home and acres of land in a tiny hamlet in the Catskills called Big Indian. The house had no central heating, no running water and no electricity. We would go up in the winter when the snow was high. It was something like a Norman Rockwell painting of a boy's dream. The first time I went we drove up from Rockville Centre in the afternoon of a cold February day — probably Lincoln's or Washington's Birthday. In the pitch dark of the early evening, we turned off the quiet main road onto a snow-covered single lane which led to the property. A few miles up the lane we stopped at a small general store — straight out of a cowboy movie — a big, glowing potbellied stove and a few old geezers sitting around it, playing checkers — to buy provisions for the weekend. The next morning, we had pancakes and hot chocolate for breakfast; sledded down the mountain; and for the first time I shot a 30.30 rifle — what Mr Keller called an 'elephant gun' — after being cautioned on how to position it 'so that the recoil won't dislocate your shoulder'. In the late spring, the troop packed onto the Keller's yacht for a day on the ocean with a barbecue on a tiny island near the shore.

My affinity to the Protestants was reinforced when my parents (together with our cousins, the Brookfields) decided to send my cousin Billy and I to a YMCA camp on North Hero Island in Lake Champlain, Vermont for two consecutive summers when we were both eleven and twelve. Camp Abnaki was a boy's dream camp. It had been founded in 1901 and the bunks, built in the twenties, were very rustic — wooden cabins with unfinished and rough-hewn walls. There was no insulation or any amenities. Toilets were about a hundred yards distant from the cabins. There were no showers. Every Sunday morning, we went 'skinny dipping' in the lake and would scrub ourselves with bars of soap. The mess hall, the 'Long House', was large and also very rustic. It was a wonderful camp.

My cousin Billy's mother, Rhoda, had a knack for finding cheap summer camps for us. She picked a winner with Abnaki. Being a YMCA camp meant that almost all the boys were Protestants. There were a few Catholics among us. I know that because they had the option of going to Mass at a Catholic church in Burlington on Sundays. Jews had no option of synagogue. Not that my cousin and I cared. However, we were required to participate in the services on Sunday, as well as Vespers every evening and Matins in the morning. 'Lights out' was accompanied by Perry Como singing 'Ave Maria'. I learnt the Lord's Prayer, the Doxology and all the hymns. I still remember many of them to this day.

We rode horses across the meadows and learned to shoot

.22s and bows and arrows (unfortunately not at the same time, which I would have loved). We took a canoe trip up Lake Champlain to Montreal, singing Onward Christian Soldiers and other rousing hymns as we paddled our twelve-man Indian war canoes. On the way, we slept outdoors on a small island in the northern part of the Lake and saw, for the first time, the Aurora Borealis. A folk singer, nicknamed 'Toto' (like Dorothy's dog), came to camp one evening a week and first introduced me to folk music. We sat around a campfire as he played his guitar, and we sang songs like 'Michael Row your boat ashore' and 'The Wabash Cannonball' — one of my favorites. After I learned to play guitar (but not as good as I remember his playing), I sang the songs I heard from him.

Every morning at the same time, a Rutland Railroad freight train would pass very close by the camp. We would count the freight cars. Some of the trains had as many as a hundred cars. They were carrying milk and dairy products from Vermont across the lake (on causeways and trestles) to New York and Canada. In fact, the end of the line was Ogdensburg, NY. I was surprised to learn (after Googling it) that Camp Abnaki still exists and is close to celebrating its 120th Birthday.

As I got older and reached *bar mitzvah* age, my affinity to Protestants weakened and although I didn't become more religiously observant, I identified more with my Jewishness. A significant impetus to this was the Adolf Eichmann capture in 1960 and his trial in 1962. I was very proud of Israel's ability to identify and grab him in Argentina, where he was living under a false identity, and spirit him away to Israel, totally undetected by the Argentinian state. The trial reintroduced me to the horrors of the Holocaust which, as I have previously written, I was aware of, but not in the detail that emerged from the trial. I hung on every word. The evil of his actions and his seemingly cold and unrepentant demeanor awakened a renewed revulsion toward the German nation. It's dominant religion — Protestantism and its clergy's complicity in the horrors committed by the German nation made me cringe. It's also possible that the trial and especially the prosecutor's skillful questioning of the accused pushed me towards the profession I would eventually follow.

Chapter 9
Guanajuato, Mexico

My attachment to my people was further reinforced when I was fifteen. My cousin Rhoda had found a summer program that was organized by a couple that she knew from Great Neck. They took a small group of fifteen- and sixteen-year-old boys and girls from the New York area to Mexico for six weeks. We were to be based in Guanajuato, a mountainous state in northern Mexico. In the end, my cousin Billy didn't join the trip. I went alone. The price of the program was more than my parents could afford, but they managed to convince the organizers that I should go as a translator. Up to that point I had taken three years of Spanish in junior high and high school and spoke it fairly well. The tour organizers agreed, but because of the cost, I couldn't stay with the rest of the group in their hotel. They made arrangements for me with a landlady who had a large house near their hotel and who rented rooms and provided meals to students at the university there. We were also enrolled in the Universidad de Guanajuato for the summer. The classes were in Spanish and many American university students, especially from Texas, which wasn't that far away, took courses there.

As I approached the front door of the hacienda where I was to be staying, I saw a large sign with big bright red letters. It read: '*Esta casa es catolica. Los comunistas no se*

entran!'
"This house is Catholic. Communists keep out!"

The Long Island I had grown up on was nothing like this. During elections, some people would put a sign with the name of their favored candidate on the front lawn, but people didn't yet express their political opinions in signs — and certainly not in such an uncivil tone. I didn't know what to expect inside.

From the outside, the house looked quite dilapidated. But that was just a façade. On the other side of the front door were porticos going off in three directions and off the porticos were bedrooms. There were probably fifteen to twenty bedrooms in the house. There was an unroofed courtyard in the middle. The courtyard was verdant and filled with palm, mangos and other tropical fruit trees. On the far side of the house — making up the fourth end of the enclosure was the dining room and kitchen. Meals were communal and quite good. I remember eating steak and French fries almost every lunchtime, which was the main meal of the day.

The other inhabitants of the house were Catholic with the exception of one student, a Muslim from Saudi Arabia.

The sign surprised me when I first saw it, and I understood it to mean that the owner of the house was Catholic and didn't like communists because they were atheists. Actually, the sign meant more than that. It meant that the house was right wing and even violently so. The students who lived there were what we might call today 'neo-Nazis'. They loved swastikas and Adolf Hitler. They had copies of 'Mein Kampf' and 'The International Jew' by Henry Ford in Spanish. They were quite friendly, when I first met them, and they proudly showed off their books and guns and bombs. I had no idea that Mexico was a place seething with political unrest. The tour leaders hadn't mentioned anything of the sort to us. No brochure from the Mexican Ministry of Tourism mentioned it. After my first lunch, the guys invited me to hang out with them during the siesta. There were about twenty of us. They wanted to know about me. I told them about myself and mentioned that I was Jewish — which now seems a bit foolish, but I was fifteen and somewhat reckless. I also mentioned that I was on the wrestling team in high school (I was only junior varsity). On the spot, one stocky student challenged me to a wrestling match. I lost, but I acquitted myself well enough that they literally gave me the thumbs up, and my Jewishness was now totally fine with them. (I was, most likely, the first Jew any of them had met and since I didn't fit the stereotype that they had of Jews — whatever that was — they treated me as one of them). In 1963, communists were not very popular in the United States and my parents, though liberal, were anti-communists, so I was too. I sort of fitted in, except for the Neo-Nazi stuff, which I argued about with them.

I learned something from them. Many people who are anti-Semitic are only so because they never met a Jew and heard stories or read books caricaturing Jews as this or that. The best way to counteract anti-Semitism is by interacting with anti-Semites. At least that's the lesson I came away with. Looking back on things, I know that lesson isn't a universal one, but in some cases and circumstances, it's true.

Because I was much younger than they were, they protected me during the brawls we had with the left-wing student houses almost every evening after leaving the *cantina* we frequented. Each house formed a sort of gang that was based on political affiliation. The violence was minimal and while one of my housemates carried a pistol hidden in his waistband, he didn't use it during my stay there. Knives and brass knuckles were the weapons of choice. I bought a stiletto (fulfilling another dream of mine) and carried it around, but never used it to harm anyone.

In the morning I went to the university where I studied in the summer school. It was all in Spanish and I really felt that I gained fluency. I don't remember all the courses we took, but much of it was Mexican history before the coming of the Spaniards, the culture of the various indigenous groups, their religions, science, technology, sociology and their agricultural practices. It was interesting, but I had other interests. Every morning before school started, I would go to a bakery near the university and buy delicious little pastries and coffee and eat them before class. Native women would be making tortillas on the street of the town, and I would buy some of them to eat for breakfast. They were cheap and delicious. As I mentioned, there were quite a few students from Texas. I had never met a Texan before, but the girls were the most beautiful I had ever seen — tall, slim, blonde, blue eyed. I got up the courage to speak to one of them. She was as sweet as she was beautiful. Adding to the magic, she was from Sweetwater. How different they were from the Jewish princesses that I grew up with on Long Island. I resolved to visit Sweetwater one day. I never did.

Every afternoon in the summer it rained at approximately 2:30pm for about twenty minutes. Then the sun came out again. When I say it rained, I mean a torrential downpour. Guanajuato is built on a mountain slope and flash floods would sweep the streets for that period. It was dangerous to be outside. After the rain we would go to a local café for a beer. With the smell of the ripe mango trees in the air after the rain and the taste of the beer — Tres XXX — Mexico was a paradise, for the fifteen-year-old me.

Chapter 10
Birth of Deena Rochel and the Cuban Missile Crisis

In the summer of 1959, my mother announced to my brother and me that she was pregnant and was expecting a baby in February. I was eleven and my brother was seven. I was concerned at first, because I was constantly being told that we had very little money and lived on a tight budget, so I couldn't understand how we could afford another child, but when Deena Rochel was born, my concerns evaporated. I was crazy about my little sister, and that bond between us grew until I left for Spain after college.

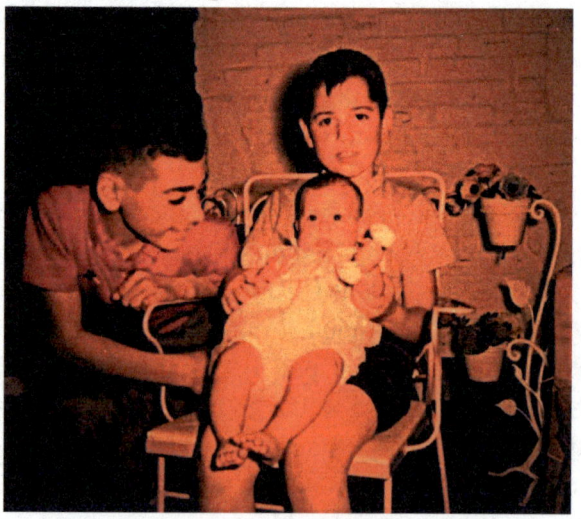

My brother and I with baby sister, Deena Rochel. Circa 1961.

The concern about money was something that haunted me as a child. In some respects, it has continued until today. As I mentioned earlier, the Depression wiped out Grandpa Semenow's business and wealth. This was a story that left a huge impression on my young mind. And it was reinforced by our yearly visits to Mount Pleasant, Westmoreland County, Pennsylvania. I associated the Depression with that town. It was a crumbling and depressing place. Located in coal country, the smell and the smoke of sulfurous fumes pervaded everything. The wooden homes were small and shabby — paint peeling off their exterior walls; metal fences were rusted and broken; the stores on the main street were aged and blackened with coal dust. I couldn't really imagine a place bleaker than this, yet during the Depression, it must have been. My overactive imagination could conjure up scenarios of our family living in a deserted and depressed Long Beach or Rockville Centre — all because we spent money too freely on unnecessary frills and didn't save. My father constantly reminded me to turn off lights when I left a room to save on electricity. Every expense was seriously examined. Was it really necessary? Could one do without the new shirt or pair of pants? How much of this was my father's insistence on saving money or my imagination of driving the family to ruin if I asked for money to buy some unnecessary item, I don't know. It's not that we lacked anything. We didn't. We ate well and lived in a beautiful house, went on a weekly outing to a restaurant and went on vacations. It was a mindset communicated to me but not to my siblings. I also became frugal. With the money I got for my allowance, meant to be spent on lunch at school, I would buy two chocolate chip cookies and a pint of milk and save thirty cents a day. That way, every few weeks I could splurge and buy myself a box of Del Monte dried apricots — my favorite food. I would never think of asking my parents for such a luxury. My mother wasn't quite as frugal as my father. Her family didn't suffer during the Depression. But she didn't spend money unnecessarily, unless it was to go to the opera, the theater, or the New York Philharmonic and that money probably came from her parents.

I started to become conscious of politics in the late fifties. My parents were Adlai Stevenson Democrats. They didn't like the young upstart, Jack Kennedy. After he won the Democratic Primary in 1960, they reluctantly supported him as the lesser of two evils. There was no way they would vote for Nixon. At twelve, I was also aligned with my parents' political preferences. Those years, the early sixties, reinforced my fatalistic outlook on life. In fact, being a member of a Boy Scout troop, which met in the basement of the local Congregational Church, I could almost see myself becoming a Calvinist. Some of us were predestined to go to Heaven and most of us would go to Hell, and it really didn't matter what you did in this life. A popular song at the time was Doris Day's '*Que sera, sera*' — 'whatever will be will be'.

A feeling of despair entered my world soon after the election of 1960. First came Strontium 90. This was a result of above ground atmospheric nuclear testing. Because of the testing, there was a cloud of radioactivity that was traveling around North America. It seemed to particularly like Minnesota, Wisconsin and North Dakota, where there was a big dairy industry. If you drank milk, you'd ingest radioactive Strontium 90 and die of cancer. My mother stopped buying milk and we drank powdered milk instead. It tasted terrible, but what could you do if you didn't want to die?

Why didn't the Strontium 90 enter the powdered milk supply? I didn't know but thought that it was because powdered milk was very old, produced years before nuclear testing — another reason it tasted so bad. We drank that watery and lumpy stuff for two years, until the radioactive clouds had sufficiently dissipated. Then came the Cuban Missile Crisis. I was in tenth grade and so convinced that the world was going to end before I finished the first term of school, that I didn't do any of the reports that were assigned to us in English or History. Why waste the effort? I felt a bit relieved, but also slightly disappointed, when the crisis was averted. I had very little time in which to write my papers.

It's interesting to think about the long-term effects of the Cuban Missile Crisis on teens like me. Nuclear war seemed a distinct possibility. Popular songs at the time included *'Where Have All the Flowers Gone'*, and the satirical Mad Magazine's take off *'On the Street Where You Live'*. Films and books like 'Dr Strangelove', 'On the Beach', and 'Lord of the Flies' made their deep impressions on my young psyche. There were bomb drills and people were advised to build bomb shelters in their backyards. The prevailing mood in those days was very bleak. The world was a menacing place filled with Nazis and Communist Russian agents — all wanting to kill us without any consideration for the apocalypse that was waiting for them too. Perhaps it's no different today. Depending on where they live, kids are concerned about mass killers, some even classmates, with access to vast arsenals, invading their schools; the environment; pollution; global warming; scarcity of clean water; or regional conflicts where death is a constant, irrational and indiscriminate reality.

Maybe it's part of Man's DNA. In ancient times Man was afraid of attacks by wild animals and neighboring tribes or kingdoms looking to expand their territory. War was often a winner-take-all game with the vanquished often slaughtered. One can see how this might contribute to a healthy state of mind. Why get upset over the minor insults and injustices of daily life when life itself is so precarious? Be nice to others because everything else is beyond your control. Don't worry about your future. You might not have one.

Chapter 11
Junior High and High School

Both the junior high school and high school were called 'South Side'. I suppose this name was given because Rockville Centre is on the south side of Long Island. But, then again, many towns and villages were located there too. Most of them bore the names of their town or village.

The junior high was near the center of town. It was a short walk from there to my father's store. I would often go to the store after school and ride home with him. Unlike elementary school, there were different academic tracks in junior high. There was one for students who were planning to go to college and another for those who weren't. Until that time, I had assumed that eventually all kids would be going to college. In homeroom of seventh grade, we sat alphabetically. The boy in the chair behind me was Howard Tully. He was planning to become an ambulance driver. His father was one and so were his brothers. He didn't need much schooling. If it weren't for state mandated education until sixteen, he would have left school long before.

The non-academic kids spent a good part of their day in the machine shop, learning how to fix cars. There were also juvenile delinquents — kids who seemed to be on a fast track to a life of crime. They started learning the business in school. Every day I, along with many other Jewish kids, would be robbed of our lunch money, or at least part of it. They would talk loudly and in detail about their conquests of the girls in our school. There was one particular conversation that I overheard in the lunchroom that has stayed imprinted in my brain. One of these 'hoods' as they were called, was bragging to his friends about torturing a cat.

"I got some string, made a noose and put it around his neck and tied the other end to a sapling; bent the sapling towards the cat and then tied his tail to another tree. I soaked him with gasoline, set him on fire and then let go of the sapling. His head popped off his body as it burned. Ha, Ha, Ha!!!" His friends laughed with him and told him that what he did was genius. I was horrified.

Aside from the 'shakedowns' of lunch money, the 'hoods' also tried to assert their budding manhood, by challenging others to fight. One afternoon I was walking to my father's store from school. I had to pass a candy store that was a 'hoods' hangout. One of them, John Croft, saw me coming towards him and challenged me to a fight. I had no reason to fight him. We had no relationship, and I had certainly never offended him in any way. But he was surrounded by friends and, I guess, felt the urge to beat someone up to show them his prowess. I didn't relish the thought of getting beaten up and improbably and spontaneously made a speech that spared me his wrath.

"John, I said, "What's the point of fighting me? I admit that you can beat me up. But what will you prove? Why don't you pick on somebody your own size" (the truth is, I was probably taller than him). For whatever reason, it worked. Probably because no one had ever answered him in that way, and he was confused and let me go.

There were other causes of anxiety at school. There were a great many rules regarding hair and dress. Woe to the student who came late to school; or who didn't have his shirt tucked in; or his hair was uncombed; or who walked in the hallways during class hours without a pass; or who went up the down staircase or down the up. Mrs Rioux, the assistant principal, kept a sharp eye peeled for the violator, who would get a severe and loud reprimand, detention and a note to be signed by a parent.

When I was in eighth grade it was discovered that I needed glasses. It never occurred to me that the fact that I couldn't see writing on the blackboard from the back row meant something was wrong with my vision. I assumed no one could. I think it was my math teacher who told me to go to an eye doctor and get my vision checked. I had to get out of my chair to get closer to the blackboard to write down the homework. I got glasses and the result was amazing. With my new glasses I could now see the blackboard perfectly from the back row. But there was a downside. I now saw that the math teacher's face was covered in deep pockmarks. Before glasses he had looked handsome, now he looked hideous.

Junior high wasn't all bad. The boys had to take 'shop'. The girls took 'home economics' (mostly cooking, sewing and household budgeting). Shop meant Photography — learning to take photographs and develop the negatives; Pottery — taking raw clay and cutting it with a wire to get all the air bubbles out and then making stuff, like ashtrays and putting a glaze on them and firing them in a kiln: Printing — using a movable metal type and a composing stick to make calling cards: Leather working — cutting the leather, working it, stamping, embossing, dyeing, attaching grommets. I made a key case with an embossed front. The last thing we learnt was using a lathe for woodworking.

I don't believe public schools do this any more. Some of the activities are antiquated and dangerous and parents are much more litigious. But in those days, it was deemed important to get a sense of the various skills needed to be an artisan or an artist, perhaps to gain a greater appreciation for those who work with their hands. Or maybe the reason was to expose the student to a trade that he might want to follow instead of continuing with an academic education. In any case, I think most of the Jews in the school saw it in the first way.

Chapter 12
Jack Average

When I was in tenth grade my parents sat me down in front of the TV to watch a 'documentary' about 'Jack Average', a senior in high school who was applying to college. It showed how the admissions office of various colleges would evaluate Jack's application. My parents told me to watch this show carefully, because, "This is about you — Jack Average."

It's amazing to me now, how my parents' words stung me.

In retrospect, I don't know if my parents really said those words. Maybe I just inferred them from the situation. Since the show was about 'Jack Average' applying to college by my parents suggesting that I watch it, it entered my memory as them saying those hurtful words. The truth is that I never had any reason to believe that my parents thought of me as 'average' — which I interpreted as below par. They were proud of my accomplishments. They were always encouraging, although not effusive in praise, as is so common today. To tell your child that whatever normal or unremarkable thing they did was 'amazing' and that they are 'amazing' — that wasn't the language of the world I grew up in. It's also not the language I employed in my own parenting. I thought that by telling a child that they were 'exceptional' or a 'genius' or some other superlative, the child would get a 'swelled head' and lead to an egotistical personality — certainly not a good thing. Maybe I was wrong. Maybe kids naturally suffer from low self-esteem and a parent must do all they can to counteract that. But I don't really believe this. Although I think my children do.

That kids can misinterpret or misremember what a parent says is certainly true. When one of my girls was a young teenager, I was heavily involved in matchmaking. I occasionally described to my family the type of people I met in that capacity. One girl was rather fat, and I mentioned to my kids one night at dinner that I had met a really nice girl, but it was going to be hard to set her up because she was very overweight. My daughter remembers me telling her that if she, my daughter, didn't lose weight she'd never find a husband. I'm positive I never said anything of the kind, and I don't recall ever thinking that my daughter was overweight, but that's how she remembers the conversation. Over twenty years later she still blames me for that 'comment'.

Jack had a B average in high school and was a member of the marching band. He was also an average athlete with at least one varsity letter. He sent applications to three colleges. I don't recall the other two, but the one he was accepted to was the University of Rhode Island. I didn't want to go to the University of Rhode Island. I knew nothing about it except that now I knew it was for average students.

There were some things that I had in common with Jack. I was an average athlete. I was on the wrestling team in the winter and the track team in the spring. I was a fairly good tennis player and loved golf, baseball and football. But I didn't think of myself as a Jack Average. I was a decent student with a B+/A- average. Maybe my parents were using a form of reverse child psychology on me to get me to work harder. But, then again, maybe they really thought I was average. In any case this bothered me. In order to avoid my 'average' fate, I worked hard to do extracurricular activities and in eleventh grade I was elected the president of the Biology Club. I was in the orchestra and marching band, in which I played an indifferent French horn. By the time I was in eleventh grade I was the second chair French horn. The first chair was extremely serious about his playing and bought a new instrument, rumored to be the best in the world, which had to be smuggled from East Germany. He was planning to be a professional French horn player and took lessons from the principal French horn player in the New York Philharmonic Orchestra. He was also the drum major in the marching band because marching around while playing the French horn would ruin his embouchure. I was not as talented or as motivated as he was. By reason of seniority, I was first chair in my senior year. I really disliked the marching band. We had to march in the cold and the rain at football games, village parades, and the county fairs. The French horn parts were mostly oompah, oompah. Not real music. One high point came in eleventh grade when we played at the New York Pavilion of the 1964 World's Fair in Queens. I joined other clubs and was the archery counselor in a summer camp. I did well enough on my SATs and got a New York State Regents Scholarship, which paid my tuition to a state school. In the end, I went to a state university. I don't think my extracurricular activities had any effect on my acceptance. I could have devoted all that time to knife throwing.

When I was sixteen, I had my first kidney stone attack. At about five a.m. on a spring morning, I felt uncomfortable and started tossing and turning in my bed. I had a pain in my back.

I tried to fall back asleep, but the pain steadily grew. Finally, I got out of bed and felt an urge to urinate. A steam of bright red blood was coming out of me. I was in horrible pain and thought I was dying. I woke up my parents and told them. By this time, the pain was so intense that I was crying and moaning. Our family doctor lived next door and my mother called him and told him what was happening to me. It was now about six-thirty a.m. About forty-five minutes later the doctor showed up.

"What took you so long? she asked.

"A man's gotta eat his breakfast," he answered in his fake laconic southern drawl.

After college in the thirties, Dr Rosenberg wanted to go to medical school, but there was a very limited quota for Jews in US medical schools. Instead, he went to Germany to study medicine and graduated in 1938. During the war he was stationed in Charleston, South Carolina where he met his wife, a Protestant Southern belle, from a military family — all of whom had gone to the Citadel — the West Point of the South. They married and after his military service he moved to Rockville Centre where he opened his office. All traces of his Judaism were hidden. They even had a Christmas tree and a Christmas party that we would attend. The only remnant was his Jewish surname, which for some reason, he kept. He had a number of sons — all of them went to the Citadel for college and became doctors and military officers. They didn't celebrate Jewish holidays, only the Christian ones. At the time I didn't know the *halacha* (Jewish law), but, in fact, his children weren't Jewish. The doctor became so *goyishe* that he even adopted his wife's pronounced Southern accent, which got thicker and thicker every year.

Whatever his personal deficiencies were (and my mother let him know what a callous and selfish attitude he had), he quickly ascertained that I was experiencing a kidney stone attack. He prescribed a strong painkiller and after a couple of hours of drug induced calm and gallons of water and cranberry juice, I passed the stone, which was later determined to be of calcium oxalate. It was crystalline and had many sharp edges, which sliced into my urethra as it passed through the urinary tract, causing the blood and pain. Since that stone I've experienced at least forty more attacks.

The next summer, the family took an epic six-week trip to the West. I don't know how my father was able to leave the business for that chunk of time, but he managed. Summer was a bit of a slow season in the dress store, and he had a good manager. I was apprehensive about traveling because of the stones, but my parents convinced me to come. It was worth it. We flew to LA and rented a car. We visited Disneyland and other attractions in LA. I was absent for a bunch of them, because I was in the motel room writhing in pain from another stone attack. Fortunately, that was the last one of the trip. We drove up from LA to San Francisco on US 1, the coastal route at a very leisurely pace. I never saw anything as beautiful in my life. The views were breathtaking — magnificent cliffs high above the Pacific; beach towns, as yet unspoiled by the blight of high-density development and yuppies; the Napa Valley and its wine country and lush vegetation. I couldn't envision a more idyllic place to live.

In San Francisco we visited with my mother's first cousin, Marty, who lived in Berkeley. He was a nuclear physicist at the Lawrence Livermore Labs there. He was quite conflicted about his work. While he didn't tell me what he did exactly, it was work for the US government and I assumed it had something to do with weapons. I got a tour of the labs and a ride in his Porsche convertible. We went to his house on a Sunday and empty gallon bottles of wine were strewn all over the floor. He told us that he had hosted a *Shabbaton* for Rabbi Shlomo Carlebach that past Friday night and hadn't had time to clean up. The next year we heard that Marty had a nervous breakdown and was hospitalized. It apparently had to do with his job. When he was released from the hospital, he quit his work at the lab and started an auto parts business. I was disappointed. My cousin the physicist was now selling auto parts. I recently heard from my second cousin, Eliot, who was Marty's nephew, that Marty actually became a very successful businessman.

Chapter 13
College

The State University at Stony Brook was in its first years when I was a freshman in 1965. The college had moved from Oyster Bay to Stony Brook in 1962 and the student body was quite small. The campus was windswept and barren. Most of Suffolk County was potato fields in those days and, I suppose that the four-hundred-acre campus had been a potato field as well. The land was denuded of any visible vegetation except for some clumps of grass here and there. When it rained the ground turned to mud. There were perhaps a few thousand students and it seemed that most of the students were in the graduate science and engineering departments. Because of its proximity to Brookhaven National Laboratories and the university's stellar physics department (we had three Nobel Prize physicists on staff and our President, John S. Toll, was also a well-known physicist) we attracted a lot of Subatomic Particle Physics students. Many of them were Chinese. There was a joke on campus that unless you spoke Chinese you couldn't study graduate physics there because the classes were in Chinese. One of the Nobel Prize physicists on the faculty was C.N. Yang who was from Taiwan.

In those days, most colleges required their undergraduates to get a well-rounded education and science and math were part of the curriculum. We were fortunate to be exposed to world class scientists and mathematicians, as well as famous writers like Phillip Roth and Alfred Kazin, who were also visiting members of the faculty.

My first year of college was a real change for me. At home, I had always had my own room to sleep in and now I had to share a dorm room with five other guys and a common bathroom for the whole floor. There were three bunk beds in the room. I took a top bunk, not knowing that the bottom bunk was the preferred choice. My roommates were mostly from the Boroughs of Brooklyn and Queens. One was from Valley Stream and one, Joe Beauregard, the only non-Jew, was from someplace in upstate New York. I was never homesick. I had spent enough time away from my parents while in Mexico or in sleepaway camp. Rockville Centre was about an hour's drive from the campus, and I enjoyed my parents' periodic visits. There were some excellent restaurants in the area, and it was a treat to eat very good food. I enjoyed my independence and freedom to explore my surroundings. I would ride my bicycle almost every afternoon, sometimes with friends, but mostly alone to the surrounding towns, Port Jefferson and Stony Brook. If it was to Port Jefferson, I'd usually have an ice cream soda at the ice cream parlor there. In Stony Brook, I usually ended up in the eighteenth-century Episcopal church (which was always open) and I would play their equally ancient organ. I don't remember studying too much, but I was fairly responsible and almost always finished my assignments on time.

 I started changing in different ways. While until that point in my life I had been somewhat competitive, I now mellowed out. I didn't care about the rewards of accomplishment. I wanted to learn things, but it wasn't in order to go to a good graduate school so that I could have a financially rewarding career. It was to learn things that would enrich my life. One could say it was learning for learning's sake. I considered my time in class either enriching or boring depending on the quality and attitude of the professor. If the class was boring, I would tune it out or not attend. I always read the material so that I could do well on the final exam, but I didn't need college for that. I have memories of one of my Anthropology professors droning on and on, week after week about how certain tribes in South America cultivated *cucurbita mixta*. He had written a book about South American pumpkins and considered this to be the most relevant subject to impart to us undergraduate Anthropology majors. I was much more interested in blow guns and poison arrows. But what could I do? I daydreamed in his class and doodled.

One of the best professors I had while in college was P. J. Staudenraus. He was a professor of American History from Wisconsin and one of the first Mid-Westerners I met. He had a dry wit, an air of modesty and a laconic way of speaking that endeared him to me. He knew his subject inside and out. I took every course he taught and hung on his every word. Most of them were about the Civil War or the period leading up to it. I was particularly impressed with him because he didn't assign his own works as required reading — forgoing the chance to make a profit on us. A couple of years out of college, while I was living in Spain, I wrote a long letter to him about Modern European History, which I was very interested in at the time. His wife wrote me back a very nice letter encouraging me in my studies and informing me of the untimely death of her husband. I felt bereft.

I made many friends in college. And while my friends and I in high school also were interested in ideas and talking about them, the reading required in college deepened our understanding and knowledge so that discussions became more intense and more educated. One of my roommates was a communist. Not a weekend one, but a really committed and knowledgeable communist. While I had read *Das Kapital*, he knew it backwards and forwards and every other major work of Marx and Engels. He was also well versed in the German Philosophy of Kant and Hegel. We argued for hours and hours almost every day. As much as I disagreed with him, I enjoyed our arguments immensely and learnt from him. With other friends I went to the horse races at Aqueduct and on adventures to Greenwich Village. We knew Yoko Ono before she was famous. She was trying to be a poet. She was terrible.

Music was a major influence. This was the time of the Beatles, Bob Dylan and about a hundred other great artists. We listened for hours upon hours to their latest outputs. One of our favorite groups was Andy Warhol's Velvet Underground. They were little known at the time and very different from anyone else. But mesmerizing — especially Nico, whose voice was haunting.

My English Teacher and the Vietnamese War

The Vietnam War period was a time of growth and development. Not all growth and development is positive. I was in my late teens and early twenties during that war. It had a major impact on me. We're used to thinking of the ones who fought and died in Vietnam as the veterans of that war and those of us who avoided or were excused from service as the 'draft dodgers'. But the truth is that we were all veterans. We were all scared, scarred and conflicted. Those of us in college, and afterwards those graduate programs that were still awarded exemptions from the Army, were safe for the time being, but the war seemed never ending and sooner or later your number would come up and you'd be sent to the jungle to die. And for what? To save Southeast Asia from the "domino effect" of communism?!! Even if one thought that communism was an evil that was sweeping the world, did we think that by fighting the Viet Cong and the North Vietnamese we would be stopping the communists from taking over America? I didn't know anyone who seriously held that opinion. South Vietnam was well known as an extremely corrupt state. Was it worth our blood and money to keep the dictators in power? Even if you believed it was a good cause, was it a cause to die for? Not unsurprisingly, I didn't think so.

In good part, my Freshman English Composition professor, Miss Ruth Michaelman, influenced my thinking about the war. In fact, the major benefit of my college experience was learning how to think and write coherently. Although I had been a good student and competent writer in high school, Freshman English was like a writer's boot camp and Miss Michaelman was an intellectual drill sergeant. She was merciless with her red pencil — calling us to task with our incomplete and run on sentences. Ideas had to be clearly thought out and expressed in a concise and clear way. My thinking, until then, had often been vague and muddled. It now had to be clear and consistent. In junior high school, English was my worst subject. I disliked my English teachers; hated grammar and could not, for the life of me, understand why an outline of an essay or paper was needed before beginning to write. It was extremely boring, seemed irrelevant and I didn't pay much attention.

In Freshman English I started to understand the purpose of an outline and the function of grammar. In fact, by the time I graduated I had taken all the linguistics classes offered at Stony Brook, including all the graduate courses. I loved grammar and language. It was historical, cultural, philosophical and mathematical. It was like a portal into the collective mind of man.

Miss Michaelman had done her undergraduate and master's degrees in English at the University of Michigan. She had also been a member of Students for a Democratic Society (SDS), an extreme leftist movement. Until I got to college, I considered myself a patriotic American and didn't really question the motives of my government. She introduced me to the idea that Big Business had its tentacles in every corner of the government — influencing government policy, particularly when it came to foreign policy. She asked me if I knew that US Rubber, Inc. had vast rubber plantations in Southeast Asia. I didn't know.

"Do you really want to die for US Rubber?" she asked.
    Of course, I didn't.

I assumed what she told me was true. I didn't ask her for proof. I see from research that I've done since that this was not a fact. But it was good enough for me. I wasn't going to go.

Towards the end of my freshman year of college I applied to be a member of the Polity Judiciary (the University Supreme Court). A few applicants at a time were called into a conference room. We were given a hypothetical set of facts and asked by faculty members to analyze them and come up with a verdict. I guess I did well enough that the faculty committee chose me to be one of the nine members of the Court. The next year they appointed me the Chief Justice. I was flattered and my girlfriend at the time gave me a real judge's gavel as a birthday present. I called the court to order and presided over it.

The cases that came to us were mostly minor infractions of the rules of the university — like disorderly conduct, or property damage. In one case, the campus police gave a ticket to a student for parking illegally. It was that student's fifth or sixth violation of the same offense. The maximum penalty could have been expulsion from the university. This student's family apparently had money and hired a Park Avenue lawyer to represent him. We were amused by the sight of this fancy and impeccably dressed lawyer standing in front of nine college kids in jeans and short sleeves trying to impress us with his oratory and legal reasoning. We stuck to the facts, disregarded the attempt at obfuscation by his lawyer and convicted him of the offense. We levied a stiff fine and told him that if he repeated his offense again, he would be expelled.

The most memorable case we had was one I was totally unprepared for. In 1968 a number of campuses in the US erupted in violent protests. This was part of a general upheaval of students around the world. In the US, the protests were mostly against the status quo, Vietnam, the 'police state', etc. There were riots at Columbia University and UC Berkeley. Buildings were occupied, police were attacked, and it seemed that 'the revolution' was starting. This was the era of Joan Baez and Bob Dylan and many other anti-establishment icons. It was also the era of Timothy Leary who preached: 'Turn on, tune in, drop out'. The drug scene was particularly strong in colleges.

In the early morning of January 17, 1968, Stony Brook was the target of the largest drug bust in the history of Suffolk County. I remember that night very well. At around twelve a.m. I was in the basement of my dorm doing laundry and a uniformed officer (he looked like a cop) walked into the laundry area and seemed to be looking for something. I asked him what he was doing there. He told me that he was from the Suffolk County Fire Department and was checking to see if the fire extinguishers were properly placed and operative. It seemed odd to me that he was doing this job in the middle of the night, but I could understand why a surprise inspection would be at an unusual hour. Later I learned the truth. He wasn't there for the fire department. He was a cop who was scouting out the venue for arrests.

At five a.m. one hundred and thirty-five Suffolk County police officers with a large fleet of police cars raided the campus. They came prepared with brochures showing a map of the campus, room numbers and outrageous descriptions of the suspects ("He is known to wear the American Flag as a cape," read one description). They had search warrants and sealed indictments and fanned out throughout the campus tearing rooms apart looking for students and evidence. In the end they arrested thirty-five people, including twenty-four students. The university was in an uproar. This was the first time in the United States that a police department had invaded a college campus to carry out mass arrests for drugs. Marijuana possession of any amount was a felony in New York State and if convicted one could receive a ten-year prison sentence. This was front-page news across the country. Stony Brook was infamous.

Unsatisfied with the results of their raid, the police launched another raid a few weeks later. This time the students fought back. They threw rocks and other debris at the police. A police car was set on fire and other police vehicles were overturned. The police retreated. Many students, particularly the SDS, saw this as an opportunity to change the power dynamics on campus and they occupied the administration building for a few days. They were arrested by the campus police and brought to trial before our court — Chairman William S. Semenov presiding.

While we had never had an audience before, this trial attracted a very large and vociferous one. The accused were undergraduates, but the audience was composed of mostly liberal arts graduate students who had been leaders of the SDS at the University of Michigan and other colleges when they were undergraduates.

They interrupted me constantly with cries of, "point of order," or "point of information." I never heard of these objections and didn't know how to handle them. Seeing that I was flustered, they gave speeches attacking the judicial process and the authorities. Our faculty advisor was of no use whatsoever. When I appealed to her to help me, she told me I was on my own.

After a short recess, I decided that these 'points of order' had no place in my courtroom and told those who made them that if they shouted out another time, I would have the campus police remove them from the hall.

While we on the court mostly agreed with the political agenda of the protesting students, we couldn't condone illegal behavior. It was ordered that a letter of censure be placed in the files of the offending students and that if there was no repeat infraction they should be removed from the files before graduation. I don't recall who came up with that solution. It might have been me, but I believe it was a result of *'siyata d'shmaya'* (help from Heaven). It managed to satisfy the administration and most of the students. I don't think it was welcomed by the SDS graduate students, but, then again, they didn't harass me afterwards.

There was a larger and more 'global problem'. That was the situation of the university. I, together with the president of the student body, was called to meet with the senior members of the administration including the President of Stony Brook, Dr John Toll, for a discussion of how to address the extremely bad publicity we were receiving in the press and in the New York State Legislature. There was an article in *Newsweek* about the student upheavals on campuses in America that mentioned the drug bust and protests at Stony Brook and called us 'the Berkeley of the East'. Of course, to us, the students, that was a great compliment, but to the administration and the establishment in New York it was a great embarrassment.

I remember arguing at the meeting that we had to placate the legislature by announcing that we were taking strong measures against drug use on campus, but that we also should protest against the overly theatrical and thuggish invasion of our campus by a spotlight seeking police department. I don't recall if my suggestions were implemented. They were just a recommendation to the administration. But my private agenda was to preserve the independence and jurisdiction of the campus judiciary, which I felt was under attack. I think I accomplished that.

Dr Bell

In college, my main academic passions were American History and Linguistics. Although I majored in Anthropology and enjoyed reading about hunter/gatherers, and cultures more or less untouched by 'civilization', I dreamt of the day where I could go into some jungle and discover a tribe that had never interacted with the 'white man'; learn their language and write about their culture, family structure; political organization and beliefs. To do this, linguistics was a key component. If one knew how to systematically break down a language into its grammatical parts, one could eventually learn it. Interestingly, all human languages have the same underlying structures — sounds that represent different relationships; objects and concepts; numbering systems and emotions. One of my professors was Dr. Bell. She was a nice 'older Jewish lady' (in her late thirties). She peppered her classes with examples from Yiddish, along with other languages. She was what I would now call *'heimishe'* (homey or familiar). She had recently gotten married to Professor Bell, a linguistics professor at a different university, who was not Jewish. I think she felt a bit guilty about 'marrying out'. In any case, in the spring of my junior year, she was visibly pregnant with her first child. She was radiant. I was very happy for her as she was one of my favorite professors and, on a personal level, was very encouraging to me. She was hoping I would go on to graduate school in linguistics. I was similarly inclined.

After the summer break, one of the first things I did was to pay her a visit to find out how she and her baby were doing. I knocked on her office door and when she opened it, I said: 'Mazel Tov!! How's your baby?'

She answered me with one word, "Dead." I slunk out of her office mumbling how dreadfully sorry I was for her loss. She taught me a very important lesson that was repeated again to me in Law School, although in a different context: "On cross-examination — never ask a question that you don't know the answer to. The answer might come back and bite you."

(This important lesson was illustrated again to me in real life in the trial of Dan Reilly whom you'll read about later).

In the case of Dr Bell, the lesson was: never ask a question to someone you haven't seen in a while about a specific family member or relationship unless you already know the answer. Someone who you're asking about might be dead or divorced. This same holds true for almost any personal question, that you don't know the answer to and might embarrass or cause pain to the other.

Another example of this happened to me a number of months ago. A friend of mine was visiting from London. He happened to mention that Gavin (who had been a close friend of mine years before) had just lost his wife. I asked him:
"Do you mean Gavin, the lawyer?"
"Yes. I believe he's a lawyer."
"He's tall and balding."
"Yes. I think so."
"He lives opposite Hampstead Heath?"
"I think so, but I'm not one hundred percent sure where he lives."

Gavin was in his middle 50s and his wife, a few years younger. It was a tragedy.

I was in England a few weeks ago and called Gavin. He sounded chipper enough on the phone and his voice didn't disclose any sadness. I asked him about his work and his family, but only in general terms.

"How's your family?"
"Thank G-d, well, and yours?"
I mentioned that I was in London for a short visit and would love to see him that evening if he was free.
"I'm terribly sorry, but tonight is our wedding anniversary and I promised my wife to take her to dinner."
I was a bit confused. Maybe his wife had died a year or two ago and he had remarried.
"Of course," I answered. "Maybe another evening."

"Yes, please ring me in a couple of days, maybe I'll have time. But tonight, is our nineteenth wedding anniversary. I'm afraid I don't have time."

I was so relieved. She wasn't dead. Another Gavin had lost his wife. I'm sorry for that one too, but it wasn't someone I knew. I wondered how Dr Bell was doing. Was she still alive? Did she have any more children? If I ever bump into her again, hopefully I won't make the same mistake.

The year before I graduated from college, Ritchie, one of my roommates, who was a year ahead of me, had applied and was accepted to medical school in Barcelona. We were all aware of three main deferments for the draft — teaching, the ministry and medical school. There were also the medical or psychological deferments of 4F or 1Y. A 4F deferment was permanent; a 1Y could get you a six-month deferment. One of my roommates, Joe Beauregard, had starved himself so that he weighed less than one hundred and five pounds, the minimum weight for a recruit of his height. He looked like the pictures I had seen of concentration camp survivors. He got a 1Y. That drastic course of action seemed extremely dangerous to me and was beyond my ability. I did have a history of kidney stones and my parents had sent me to William Kuntsler, a famous New York lawyer and anti-war activist, who helped people avoid the draft legally. His office was building up a file for me as a 4F in case I needed it. I didn't relish the thought of having to go to an induction center with my medical file in case they didn't agree with my lawyer's evaluation.

I had actually gone to Fort Hamilton, in Brooklyn, with

Harvey, another of my roommates when he got a draft notice. He tried for a 1Y psychological deferment, claiming that he was a homosexual, which in those days was classed as a mental disorder. He wasn't. He asked me to go along with him and act as his boyfriend. On the bus from the parking lot to the induction office about a third of the guys were dressed in drag. Harvey was not the only one with this plan. But Harvey was smarter. He didn't dress like a girl or act like a pansy. Inside, everyone stripped to their underwear. The guys in drag also had panties and some had bras. Harvey just sobbed during the physical exam and I, who was fully dressed, because I did not get a notice, had my arm around Harvey (who was about three inches taller and fifty pounds heavier than me) and tried to calm him down.

He was lucky to get an interview with the psychiatrist. Most of the other 'homosexuals' did not. He was successful and got his 1Y. In any case, the foreboding atmosphere of the Fort and the assembly line induction further repelled me. I did not want to be in his situation.

At the time, to my knowledge, becoming a minister meant a Catholic priest or a Protestant minister. I never considered that I could become a rabbi and never knew that fifty miles away in Brooklyn there existed 'draft-dodging' *yeshivos*, where one could be enrolled and get a deferment and never have to attend. But medical school sounded good, particularly since the admission standards were lax at the University of Barcelona, compared to medical schools in the States. And the fact that it was in Spain made it sound even better. I applied along with a couple of my roommates, and we were accepted.

Woodstock

I've forgotten to mention that I am famous — at least among our oldest daughter's friends — the ones that heard of Woodstock. Yes, I was there. I've even let a few of her friends shake my hand. Among her younger siblings' crowd, I'm not so famous. It's like telling someone born in the late eighties that when you were in college LBJ was president. The reaction is usually a blank stare. Unless they went to college or were listening well in American history class in high school, they haven't heard of President Lyndon B. Johnson or the war in Vietnam. Although, Woodstock is probably more famous than either of those.

Stony Brook had a student social events and concert organizer who probably went on to make billions in the music industry. I don't remember his name, but he was a master at his craft. How he convinced the New York State Legislature or the governor or the Board of Regents to give us a gigantic budget for concerts and lectures, I'll never know, unless he writes a book. With the exception of the Beatles and the Rolling Stones I think he booked every major soloist and band in the world. We had Ravi Shankar, Richie Havens, Crosby, Stills, Nash and Young, Country Joe and the Fish, Jefferson Airplane, The Doors, Jimmy Hendricks, The Band, Blood Sweat and Tears, Chicago, Blind Lemon Jackson, Santana, Janis Joplin, etc. etc. So, I had heard almost all the groups that played at Woodstock in a more intimate setting — and being in the student government, I met some of them in person.

I'm a person who avoids crowds and wasn't planning to go to Woodstock when the organizers, youngish New York mostly Jewish entrepreneurs, first announced the idea to hold a festival for the members of our generation. It sounded like a lot of hype, and I didn't want to participate in a commercialization of my generation. But as the date neared there was a realization that this was not going to be just another 'rock' concert, but a major cultural event. That coupled with the fact that I had nothing better to do that weekend and my girlfriend wanted to go, was reason enough. The event began on Friday evening on August 15th, 1969. Woodstock is in the Catskills in an area that was surrounded by Jewish 'bungalow colonies' — rustic cabins where Jews from New York City would stay for the summer. A number of summers later my wife and I would come back to the area to be the camp directors at one of these colonies.

Bobby Delfaunt and I and our girlfriends drove up from Long Island. It's a trip that we figured would take about two and a half hours. We left at about five p.m. At about seven-thirty we hit very heavy traffic on Route 17. By eight p.m. we were about three miles from the event site and the traffic wasn't moving. It was apparently going to be a huge event. Everyone just left their cars on the road's shoulder and walked the rest of the way. As we approached the event site, Chasidim in their Shabbos clothing were lining the road leading up to the farm to see all us weirdos. We were quite tired from the hike when we finally got to the site and put down our blankets. We hadn't planned very well and while we had two blankets and some sandwiches, it wasn't enough for the three-day event. The stage was really far away, and I could barely see the performers. The speaker system was good, but not great. The Stony Brook performances were much better. There were hundreds of thousands of people, and I was claustrophobic. I felt like an idiot and wanted to go home. But that was totally unrealistic. I was stuck here for three days and had to make the best of it. We slept poorly. The ground was hard, and the night was cold, and we only had one blanket per couple. It was also hard to sleep because the music was blasting all night long. In the morning it was better. The sun rose early and warmed the earth. The music sounded clearer that day and I started feeling more a part of something. As I walked towards the port-o-johns I saw a commotion. A girl was having a 'bad trip' and was freaking out — screaming and flopping around on the ground. A stretcher appeared and I grabbed onto it and helped carry the screamer to a medical station. I was now a participating member in my generational event. This was big. My claustrophobia disappeared and we were able to move closer to the stage. I started enjoying myself.

On our hike back to the car on Monday morning, we stopped at a pancake house on Route 17 and had a big breakfast. In sharing our experiences after the event, we discovered that we had all felt the same way at the beginning. We all wanted to leave and then gradually got into it. I took a lot of pictures.

The truth is, Woodstock wasn't that big of a deal at the time. It was, at first, considered a financial failure. There were plenty of complaints because the organizers hadn't prepared properly for the number of people who showed up. There were shortages of everything from food and water to toilets. I don't know what happened to Max Yasgur's farm after the event, but the crowd certainly destroyed it while there. It probably was an environmental disaster. Woodstock only became famous in its aftermath and popularized by songs like Joni Mitchell's 'Woodstock' covered by Crosby, Stills, Nash & Young and by the movie 'Taking Woodstock'. The media played a large part in the hype. We were now called the 'Woodstock generation'.

I didn't think at the time I was participating in an iconic and historic event. But I did and that led to my fame.

Chapter 14
Spain

The following fall three of us headed off to Spain — me, Victor and Richie. Our first order of business was to find a place to live. We had researched cheap residences while we were still in New York and found a place near the Plaza Catalunya and Las Ramblas — The Pension Central. I don't recall the exact amount of rent for a month, but it was cheap. We were two in a tiny room and there was one bathroom and toilet for the whole floor of about thirty or so young people. All of the other residents were Europeans — French, German, Dutch, English and Scottish. We had a common dining room and kitchen. One German guy — Bernd, was a heroin addict, a con artist, and a petty thief. His girlfriend was a French countess, or so she said, and also a heroin addict. Their scam was to find tourists and convince them that they were on their honeymoon and that someone stole all their money. They would ask for a loan which they promised to repay as soon as they returned to Berlin and Bernd could go to his bank and send the bank transfer.

Another German, Franz, had an even better scam. He told Victor, Richie and me that he was a *graf*, a baron, and his father owned a big bank in Frankfurt. He was in Barcelona working as a banker for a local bank that did business with his father and getting experience so that he could take over his father's bank. He dressed very well and had a briefcase and seemingly went to work every day. One day he showed us photos of a large castle in Germany with a lake that he said his family owned but weren't using. They didn't know what to do with it and maybe we had some ideas. If three New York Jews couldn't figure out what to do with an idyllic castle with fifty rooms in Western Germany, who could? Why not turn it into a hotel was our considered and unanimous opinion. Franz was flabbergasted!

"I can't believe it. Of course, it's perfect for a hotel. You guys are geniuses," he exclaimed. "You'll be my partners in the hotel. My family has the money to renovate it. We'll make millions. Let's go out and celebrate. I'm inviting you to the best restaurant in Barcelona. Order whatever you like. It's on me."

Off we went and spared no expense. When it came time to pay, Franz took out his credit card and gave it to the waiter. The charge was declined. Franz insisted on speaking to the manager and told him what an outrage this was. He, the scion of a great German banking family and a baron to boot, having his credit card declined?! In the end there was nothing he could do. He didn't have any cash. He asked us to pay the tab and he'd return the money the next day, when his father wired him his monthly allowance. As they say in Yiddish, which is really German from the Middle Ages, '*a nechtage tag*' — another day — meaning, 'forget it'. Franz kept coming up with excuse after excuse as to why the transfer wasn't coming through, until one day he disappeared. We were so naïve. Why would a rich banker stay at the Pension Central — little more than a third-class flophouse? And why couldn't he figure out what to do with a property that was perfect for a hotel? We were lucky to have gotten away with paying for a good dinner and receiving a valuable lesson.

During the whole first year of medical school, I attended exactly one class. My mother made me promise that I'd go to at least one class. Maybe I'd like it and want to become a doctor. The class was called 'Histology'. The school was like ones I had seen in European movies — a big Gothic-like building. Classes were held in a giant amphitheater. The professor stood at the blackboard and lectured. That class was like high school chemistry. I was bored. That really wasn't very surprising. After all, the Spanish students, who were ninety-eight percent of the class, were only high school graduates. In Europe, like most of the world, students enter professional school from high school. They don't have to spend four years getting an undergraduate degree. I had already taken chemistry in college. I never went back to the school except to register for two subsequent years. If you failed your exams, you could just re-register for that year. The truth is that even had I wanted to go to classes the school was closed for about eight months of the years I was there because of student riots and protests. They did have exams. The students read the materials and took the exams. I was always wary of Spanish doctors after my experience. How could they be trusted to know anything if a large part of their education was self-taught? In any case, the draft board accepted the letter from the school saying that I was enrolled. It didn't say what year I was in.

During that first year in Spain, I devoted my time to photography. I had long been interested in that art form. Although I loved to draw, I wasn't very good at it.

Photography offered an alternative. I got my first camera when I was about ten years old — a Kodak Brownie. It was a very simple camera and the pictures it took weren't very good. One couldn't focus the camera, so the images weren't sharp. It was fun but also expensive and you had to wait about a week for the developed pictures to come back from the drug store. In junior high we learnt how to develop film in Shop class. It wasn't that difficult after you practiced a few times, but I didn't have a darkroom at home and no real place to make one.

My parents bought me a 35-millimeter camera for my bar mitzvah. It wasn't a fancy one, but I could focus it and change the settings depending on my light meter readings. I loved it and snapped away as often as I could. My parents paid for the developing, so I wasn't careful to make sure every shot was a masterpiece. In fact, very few were decent, but gradually their quality improved. When I graduated from college, my parents bought me a Nikkormat — the cheaper Nikon. It was a very sturdy camera and the only real difference between it and the Nikon F (which was the preferred camera for professional photographers outside the studio) was that the F had a better built-in light meter. Since I had gotten used to using a handheld light meter that difference didn't matter to me at all. Both models used the same interchangeable lenses, so the quality of the images was the same. Of course, the better the lens the more expensive it was, but one could find used lenses in good condition, and I did. Although, to be honest, I also felt a little inferior with the Nikkormat body.

At the Pension Central I met a Scot named Brian. He was a professional fashion photographer in town for a few months for a number of photo-shoots. (He owned a few cameras; one was, of course, a Nikon F). While I couldn't understand his Highland accent at first, gradually I came to understand him. He critiqued my pictures and taught me a number of very valuable lessons.

The first was that the most important thing for a photographer was a good eye for a photograph. "Ye could have the best camera in the world, but if ye haven't got an eye for a good photo, it won't do ye any good."

The second was that he thought I had a good eye for pictures.

The third was to always compose the picture in the camera. Don't rely on cropping the image afterwards. Each frame had to be perfectly composed.

The fourth was how to set up a darkroom, what black and white film to use, and how to alter the instructions on the boxes of chemicals to get a much finer grain. He was meticulous and had experimented with different concentrations and temperatures of chemicals and found the perfect formula. He shared it with me.

I moved out of the Pension Central, got a small apartment in the nearby Barrio Gotico and set up my darkroom. I also got a job with a schlocky fashion photographer and started learning what I could from him. Calling my boss, a fashion photographer, is actually a gross exaggeration. He shot portfolios of 'would be' models. Almost none of them had the slightest chance to make it as a professional. The ones that did probably went to a much better photographer than he, but it provided a living for him and his family while feeding a fantasy to a lot of ditzy girls. I wasn't interested in this type of photography but thought it necessary to 'learn the business'. I wanted to be an artist-photographer who got paid for his photographs. I soon learned that with the exception of very few photographers in the world, that wasn't a realistic goal.

In the course of my pursuit, I frequented the main photography shop used by all the professionals in town. I met a few really good ones. The best, in my opinion, was Tony Keeler. Tony was an American expat who owned a photography shop in Sitges, a beach town south of Barcelona. He was also rich and could indulge in his hobby without the concern of making a living. His photos were published in a number of European photography magazines. His specialty was photojournalism — going into a small town and taking pictures of the residents — especially the old people. His pictures were very large, black and white and very grainy. Since most of his subjects were the small villages of southern Spain, graininess was perfect for relating the hard life of the peasants in sunny Spain. I got to know Tony and learned from him how to interact with people and to photograph them. The best portraits were not the result of the photographer as voyeur or asking his subject to say 'cheese', but a real interaction with the subject. I'm reminded of the famous war portrait of Winston Churchill scowling at the camera with palpable hatred. You can almost hear him saying:

"We shall go on to the end. We shall fight in France, we shall fight on the seas and oceans, we shall fight with growing confidence and growing strength in the air, we shall defend our island, whatever the cost may be. We shall fight on the beaches, we shall fight on the landing grounds, we shall fight in the fields and in the streets, we shall fight in the hills; we shall never surrender."

I once saw a documentary about Yousef Karsh, Churchill's photographer. He described how he got that bulldog expression from Churchill. Sir Winston was smoking his cigar and being quite uncooperative. Karsh snatched the cigar from his hand and at that moment snapped the shutter.

Tony taught me that the photographer should be an active participant in the picture. He also shared with me his formula for the chemicals used in development to get that large grain.

As a result of my work with the fashion photographer, I got a job with a record company. It wasn't the kind of work that my boss did, so he was happy to give it to me. I did publicity shots for the bands that the label represented and, eventually, album covers. At that point I quit my job with the fashion photographer. I liked the new work because it allowed for my own artistic expression. This was a time when record album covers were an important part of the marketing of the band and its records. Album covers were works of art. It was before computer graphics, so the photographer was the artist. Part of my work involved selling my pictures to popular magazines. I would photograph our artists' concerts and then rush home to develop and print the pictures late at night and then run to the magazines early in the morning in order to be among the first photographers there. The magazines would only buy a few photographs of each concert, so being early was a must. I didn't like this part. I was working like a dog and running for money — definitely not what I loved about photography. After a few months of this and after a number of rejection letters from top art photography magazines in Europe for my artistic photos, I lost much of my passion for photography and slowly began to resent taking pictures unless someone paid me for them. I decided if I was ever going to be a real artistic photographer, I had to quit my job as a professional and only do it only as art. Another problem I had was getting paid. The magazines, even when they bought your photos, were very slow to pay and unless one was very aggressive at pursuing them, you'd never see a peseta. Also, my job at the record company didn't pay very well. Even if I was lucky enough to sell my pictures, that together with my job didn't pay enough for rent and food.

However, as a side benefit to my job, I became a songwriter. To be successful and famous, a European band had to sing in English. The top band that was represented by the record label was 'Machina'. It was a very popular band in Spain but almost unknown in the rest of Europe. As the only native English speaker they knew well, they asked me to write songs for them. They also asked me if I could sing and play an instrument — to be a part of the band. They did not need a French horn player. But I did play the piano and tried to play with them. However, it was soon obvious to everyone, including myself, that I was in over my head. As for the singing, I managed to do one concert, but my range was not sufficient. The band members were excellent musicians. I was not. But my lyrics were good enough. I wrote quite a few songs for them — many were recorded and played on the air. I would check, every once in a while, with the local branch of the organization of artists and performers, which handled royalties paid by radio stations. The money was paltry and after a while I stopped checking in. But, who knows, maybe I have a fortune in royalties waiting for me in some Spanish royalties office.

I don't remember many of the songs I wrote, but one went like this:

"I am a man who's wandered for at least a thousand years. My eyes have heard the sorrow and my ears have seen the tears."

Another one:

"Walking in the lush green forest, Robin Hood is by my side

Stop he says, I see a beggar sitting by yon big green beechnut.

Takes an arrow nicely fletched and threads the bow and then he lets it go. How can I see what I feel? How can I know what is real…?"

Now I'm not saying it was material for the Beatles, but for Spaniards it was fine. It rhymed and was in English.

Chapter 15
I Become a Slaveholder

I needed a "real" job and when a friend told me about an opening for an English professor at one of the most prestigious business schools in Spain (ESADE, the Escuela Superior de Administración de Empresas), I applied. My background in linguistics helped me persuade the Chairman of the English Department to hire me. The school was run by Jesuits, who are reputed to be the most intellectual and dynamic of the priestly orders. I'm convinced that had the director of the school followed a secular life he would have been a captain of industry.

I enjoyed teaching. And soon after starting the job, other offers for teaching, both privately and in businesses, came to me. Within six months or so, I was earning about four times the average wage in Spain. I rented a large three-bedroom apartment in the upscale neighborhood of Avenida Buenos Aires, which wasn't far from Mount Tibidabo and Gaudi's Art Nouveau Parque Guell. I hiked there daily and took many photographs. I set up a darkroom in one of the bedrooms. I also could now afford to eat out in the best restaurants from time to time.

One that I frequented often was the Café Soleil. The doorman there was a Black man from Cuba. He wore a red velvet riding coat and a black top hat and was very talkative. I hung out with him for long conversations both before and after dinner. Like the hobo millionaire, when it comes to people, there is often more to them than meets the eye. Miguel Penllaver y Villarverde was not just some low paid flunky opening doors at a high-end restaurant. He had been a Cuban diplomat from a pre-revolution wealthy and upper-class family in Havana. His father was a doctor, and his uncle was the Archbishop of Havana. Miguel was very intelligent, well read, and a poet. He described to me in vivid terms the crushing oppression and lack of freedom in Cuba. Since he was a teenager, he wanted to escape. To that end, he studied hard, did well in school and university and secured a place in the diplomatic corp. His first assignment was as the third secretary of the Cuban delegation in Madrid. As soon as he arrived, he defected. Spain however wasn't willing to grant him citizenship and so he had no passport. His Cuban one was, of course, immediately revoked. He was stuck in Spain. And because of his status he couldn't work legally. Therefore, he took a job with a kindhearted restaurateur —Eddy Stahl.

Another friend whom I met at the restaurant was the guitar player — Sergio Spector. Sergio was born in Egypt of a Russian-Jewish father and an Italian mother. He spoke at least seven languages perfectly, played classical guitar and knew all the latest hit songs. He had a beautiful voice. I don't remember why he was stateless, but he was and after I left Spain, he obtained travel documents from the UN and was finally able to leave Spain. At the time I knew him he was also unable to work legally and worked for Eddy at the restaurant.

When I moved into my apartment on the Avenida Buenos Aires, I had frequent get-togethers there. Miguel loved to cook and made excellent paellas; arroz con pollo and arroz Cubano.

Sergio would play guitar and I accompanied him on a bongo drum.

One evening, as we were improvising some music, Miguel stopped me and said,

"Where did you learn that beat?"

"Nowhere. It just came to me."

"That's impossible, That's the beat and rhythm of Obatala Obatala."

What's that?" I asked.

"He's the highest god of my people — the Yoruba tribe of West Africa. It's impossible that you should play like that. You must be the incarnation of Obatala Obatala."

I must say I was honored by his praise but didn't for a minute think it might be true.

Later that evening he told me that he wanted to be my slave. He would cook and clean for me. He just needed a place to sleep. I had a spare bedroom, so I gave it to him.

Since I did not affect an act of acquisition, it's not clear if I actually acquired Miguel as a slave. But if I did, slaveholding is not what it's cracked up to be. Miguel liked to cook but was very messy and rarely cleaned up after himself. I had to. He often needed money to go places and while he still worked at the restaurant it wasn't enough for his expenses. As a 'slave owner' he expected me to pay for whatever he needed. One could say he took advantage of me, but he was such a loyal friend and enjoyable companion that I didn't really mind. When I left Spain, he asked me to do what I could to get him a visa so that he could leave Spain and continue in his role as my slave in America. As much as I liked Miguel and wanted to help him, I didn't want him to come to the States where I might be held in opprobrium by others who, when introducing himself to them, might describe himself as my slave. Even had I lived in New York before Lincoln's Emancipation Proclamation it might have caused a ruckus. In New York in the 1970s and the Black Power Movement, I might have been the one lynched.

Chapter 16
Spanish Exit

Living in a right-wing dictatorship seemed mild to me compared to what I heard and read about communist dictatorships. Instead of a planned economy and food shortages, there was capitalism and plenty. While free speech was an issue for some, the government pretty much left everyone alone as long as you didn't cross them. You could say and think what you like and discuss it with your family and friends. Problems would occur if you published anti-government screeds or met in public in groups of more than three to discuss your anti-government views. Also, caricatures of Generalissimo Franco were forbidden. My wife, who was then my girlfriend, was an artist and she drew a portrait of General Franco for the cover of a magazine. As soon as it hit the streets, the government confiscated every copy. There was nothing offensive about the portrait, but it wasn't officially authorized.

In any case, as long as you weren't political you had nothing to worry about. For a citizen of Spain that would have been oppressive, but for a foreign resident, like myself, it was OK. It wasn't my country, and I didn't mind not being able to criticize it in print or in public. At least that's the way I felt for the first two years I was in Spain. By the third year, having gotten married and more settled in my lifestyle, I started to feel the lack of freedom. It was now more personal. On a visit with my wife to Mallorca, we were touring the countryside and I saw a military compound of the Guardia Civil, the feared National Military Police Force. The guards were parading with their weapons, and I thought it would make a nice photo. I got out of the car and took a couple of shots of the guards. My wife was screaming at me to come back, but before I did a guard raised his rifle as if to shoot. I failed to notice a sign that read: 'Keep off the grass'. I acknowledged my mistake and got back into the car.

"Are you crazy?" she said. "He could have shot you."

I didn't believe her. I mean not obeying a 'keep off the grass' sign was a capital offense?

"It's true. They are vicious. You are very lucky he didn't shoot. Not just for stepping on the grass, but it's absolutely forbidden to take photographs of the Guardia Civil. Everyone knows that."

I didn't photograph another guard unless I was far away and didn't think I could be seen.

Another time, I was on a bus and while I paid the fare, I had trouble locating the receipt. In those days you entered the bus from the back and purchased your ticket from the ticket seller whose station was placed in a way that it was virtually impossible to get past him without paying. Nevertheless, occasionally, inspectors would board the bus and check to see if everyone had their ticket. The tickets were printed on tiny strips of tissue-like paper. They were easy to lose and dissolved if you put them in your mouth, which might be done if you had your arms full of packages.

On that particular trip the inspectors asked to see my ticket. Because I considered the inspectors to be agents of the government, I rebelled. I told them that there was no way I could've gotten into the bus without purchasing a ticket and it was a stupid rule that required me to show the ticket. Failing to persuade them to leave me alone, I reached into a bag I carried in which there were about fifty used tickets. I took them out one by one and showed them to the inspectors. Understandably they were upset with me. But I was upset too. It was as if the heel of the Fascist state was grinding me into the ground. I wasn't going to take it. The inspectors threatened to arrest me. I wasn't scared. I yelled at them, "Take me to the police. I'm not going to take this any more." At the next stop they escorted me off the bus and told me we were going to the police station. I didn't care. In the end they let me go. Upon reflection, I realized that I was probably a danger to myself. But the system was getting to me.

It was time to leave.

I had become friendly during my first year in Barcelona with a radio disk jockey. His name was Constantino Rodriguez. He later became quite famous in Spain. He acted in movies and had his own prime time TV Show. He was the Johnny Carson or Jay Letterman of Spain. When I met him, he hosted a prime-time radio show on a station called Radio Young. As its name implies, it was marketed to the youth of Spain. Constantino played the latest in American and English music. This was the era of Bob Dylan and the Beatles, the Band, Jefferson Airplane, etc. etc. He invited me to give color in English to the latest hits. He rarely let a song play for longer than ten seconds before he or I jumped in with some comment or other. If you were a listener, it must have been quite annoying, but for me it was great fun. I loved going to the radio station, which was just down the street from the Pension

Central, at 9 pm every day for the half hour show and unofficially co-hosting the program. Constantino was from Segovia or Salamanca or some other place in Castile. He had perfect Spanish diction with a deep and resonant voice. He was in great demand as a voiceover artist and used to dub all the foreign movies. Because of our friendship he arranged gigs for me to dub actors when they wanted to keep part of the dialogue in English. Dubbing required erasing the original soundtrack, which then needed to be re-recorded for the entire movie. It was fun and well-paid work.

I kept up my friendship with Constantino even after I moved away. When we were planning to leave Spain, I decided to pay one last visit to the radio station and say goodbye to Constantino. Graciously he turned the mike over to me and told me to say my goodbyes to him and Spain and then he left the soundproof broadcasting booth and stood next to the engineer. A strange thought popped into my head at that moment. I'm sure it had to do with my frustration with the government. I said:

"Constantino has been seized by CIA agents who invaded the station just minutes ago. They are stuffing dollar bills down his throat and forcing him to become a lackey of the American government."

I could see Constantino's face drain of blood. He motioned to the engineer to cut off the sound. He wasn't angry at me when he ran into the broadcasting booth but told me that what I had done was really serious and there would be consequences for the station and for him and if I knew what was good for me, I should leave Spain that night because he was sure the police were coming for me.

We had our possessions, which were few, packed into my

Alfa Romeo Junior and left that evening, driving straight to the French border, before I could be arrested. I called Constantino the next day and apologized and asked him what happened. He told me that the police did indeed come that night, but because I had spoken in English, the station received just a reprimand from the government, but nothing more serious than that. He was fine. No action was taken against him.

Chapter 17
How I Met Your Mother

In the summer of my second year in Spain, I, along with much of Barcelona, went to the beach. For me it was Playa del Oro on the Costa Brava. Many Spaniards, except for the very poor, had summer residences on the coast. Like New York in the fifties, almost no one had air conditioning and the cities were like ovens. On the coast, one could breathe.

I got a job working for my friend who owned the Café Soleil in Barcelona. Eddy Stahl had a branch of his high-end restaurant in Playa del Oro called Le Petit Soleil and he needed a photographer to take pictures of the patrons. He asked me if I would be interested. In return, I could keep the profits from the photos, and he gave me a room in his beach apartment — rent free.

The arrangement suited me well. At this point in time, I had about a thousand dollars left to my name and couldn't afford to waste anything. After a week or so of work I decided to go into a different business. Eddy's wife owned a dress shop below the apartment. She did a brisk trade in summery dresses. After seeing a Moroccan dress in the store that had been selling particularly well, I asked if she would like to have more of them. Morocco wasn't far away and the cost of a round trip flight was around two hundred dollars, so I set out for Tangier. I had been there before during my first year in Spain and knew my way around the city. I shopped around until I found a manufacturer who gave me a good price for the dress, and I had him make up a hundred of them in different colors and sizes. Within a week I had brought them back to Playa del Oro. Mrs Stahl was willing to let me display them in the store, and she agreed to sell them on concession. Sales were slow.

One night, I was at the restaurant taking pictures and Eddy told me that he invited a girl to have dinner there with the Pakistani Ambassador to Spain — who had booked a table with specific instructions to have a pretty girl eating with him in case the press got wind of his plans and photographed him at dinner. It sounded a bit strange. I mean, why should an ambassador care about being seen eating alone at a restaurant? Maybe he thought that people would assume he was a loser to be eating alone? I don't know. In any case, he requested that the girl speak English, because his Spanish was poor. Eddy asked me to speak English with this girl for an hour or two before the meeting, so that she might practice her English. I reluctantly agreed.

My reluctance left me when I met Anna Maria. She was the most beautiful girl I had ever seen. I stammered and grasped for words. She introduced herself and the first thing she told me about her background was that she was Jewish. I almost fell off my chair. "What an amazing coincidence," I said, "I'm Jewish too."

We hit it off immediately.

Then she told me that she had been in the restaurant the night before, with an Italian friend and I had taken their picture. I had absolutely no recollection of the picture, even after she showed it to me. It turned out that it was her idea to ask Eddy to practice her English with me before her meeting the ambassador.

    The next day I asked her if she would mind modeling the dresses I bought. The dresses looked enchanting on her and I took a number of shots that I developed and printed and placed in the window of the dress store. The sales measurably increased.

Chapter 18
Marriage

On December 12, 1971, we were married on a farm near the town of Santa Cristina de Aro, in the Province of Girona, not far from Playa de Oro. The whole wedding party was only about thirty people made up of our friends and Anna's father's family. In order for the marriage to be legally registered it had to be performed by an authorized official. Spain was a Catholic country, and the Catholic Church was the only authorized body that could perform a marriage, unless neither of the parties was Catholic. Since Anna Maria came from a Catholic family, she could only be married in a church, unless she became a legally recognized apostate.

One might think that the marriage would have been an unmitigated calamity for her family. In those days for a Jew to marry 'out' was still fairly scandalous in the Jewish community, although it was a phenomenon that had been gaining attention. There was a popular network TV series in the 1972-3 season, 'Bridget Loves Bernie' which explored this topic and was canceled after one season. Even the Conservative movement condemned it. The idea of a Jew converting to another religion was almost unthinkable. But, in Anna's case, it wasn't leaving the Church that was a problem. It was the idea of her marrying a Jew.

Anna's father, Alfredo, was fine with it. He was an

intellectual, an atheist and rabidly anti-clerical. As a young man he was studying engineering at the University of Barcelona in 1936 when the Spanish Civil War began. Alfredo was from a wealthy Catalan family who were pro-Republican (the side against Franco). In fact, he had an uncle who was the senior Catalan general in the war. His father, a doctor, was also very active politically as a socialist, and was eventually imprisoned by Franco's forces and died as a result of maltreatment. Alfredo, at the age of nineteen, left school and joined the Republican Army. As an engineering student, he was one of the few men in his division who was able to decipher the manuals that came with the Russian artillery pieces that Stalin had contributed to the cause. He was made a captain and given a battalion of Artillery. By the end of the war, he was a colonel. The Spanish Catholic Church strongly supported Franco and while his family had never been religious, it now hated the Church. To Alfredo and his brothers and sisters, marrying out of the Catholic religion was a badge of honor.

Her mother's position was not similar. She was from Inca in Mallorca. Her father was a newspaper publisher and something akin to the poet laureate of Mallorca. He too was an intellectual but wasn't political. His poetry was very religious. In fact, he was considered to be the most Catholic layman in Inca. His son, Miguel, a psychologist, was pro-Republican and very involved politically. He was arrested in the early stages of the war and kept in prison for all of it. He narrowly escaped execution. He was also a rabid anti-cleric as was his sister and brother. But Francisca or Fanny, as she liked to be called, Anna's mother, was not interested in politics. She was not an intellectual. She was interested in fashion and aspired to high society. Added to this, the family had a deep dark secret.

Everyone has heard of the Spanish Inquisition. Most people think it happened in and around 1492 when Columbus (whose actual surname was Colon and who many think was a Jewish Catalan from Mallorca) set sail to discover a western route to India. The truth is that the Inquisition was actually an office of the Catholic Church that investigated (or 'inquired' into) the ideological purity of the Church's subjects. It began in the thirteenth century in France and quickly opened offices in other Catholic countries. The last office of the Inquisition only closed in 1908. It held 'trials" and burned witches and heretics. It also confiscated their property. Jews who had converted to Catholicism (usually for business reasons) were particular targets of the Inquisition. Many were insincere and continued practicing Judaism in secret. And many were rich. In 1391 a major push by the Inquisition to investigate *conversos* (converted Jews) led to mass burnings and the confiscation of their property. This happened all over Spain, but it was particularly vicious in Mallorca. It's important to remember that the Inquisition and the Expulsion of Jews are not synonymous. Jews practicing Judaism were allowed to live in Spain until 1492 when they were expelled. In the rest of the country, the converted Jews (and the converted Muslims) intermarried and blended into the general population. Not in Mallorca. It's a small island with a long memory. The *sambenitos* (the identifying aprons that the *conversos* wore to their deaths) were prominently displayed in the Cathedral in Palma together with the names of their wearers until very recently. Everyone in Mallorca knows the family names of the *conversos* and no upstanding Old Christian Mallorquin would marry into one of those tainted families.

The *conversos*, or as they are called derogatorily in Mallorquin, *marranos* or *chuetas* (pig swill), were segregated and married amongst themselves. Only within the present generation is there a weakening of this anti-Semitism. But there were families who 'passed'. One of them was the Duran family of Anna's mother. When Anna was fifteen, her uncle, the psychologist, showed her a family tree that had been secretly passed down through the generations showing they were the descendants of Rabbi Shimon Duran and of Rabbi Tzemach Duran of thirteenth century Mallorca. These men were actually among the greatest Jewish scholars in the world during their time. Their works are well known today and quoted often in all *yeshivot* and in scholarly writings. This was a source of pride to her uncle and now to her, but it was a great source of embarrassment to her mother, who desperately wanted to 'pass'. Fanny was lucky. After the war and after having been repatriated to Spain from France where he fled after Franco's conquest of Catalunya, Alfredo finished his studies (he did a doctorate in engineering) and then had to begin his unwilling, but conscripted military service in Franco's army, where he was a lowly private for three years. He was posted to an army base in Inca, and there met Fanny, who quickly ascertained that he was her meal ticket out of her drab middle-class life in her provincial town.

For Anna's mother, the prospect of her daughter marrying a Jew was almost too much to bear. I saw this first hand. I don't think she liked me too much, but she had no great hatred for me either. She seemed satisfied that her daughter probably wouldn't end up living in poverty, but the idea of marrying a Jew related to those social outcasts in her home island was too much! Besides, her mother had other plans for Anna Maria.

She was a social climber and a tad unrealistic. She actually believed that Prince Charles of England was her daughter's *bashert* (her intended marriage partner), and she was going to do all she could to make that happen. Anna went to the most exclusive private schools in Spain where most of her classmates were from noble families — some were even related to the British royal family. Her mother took her to Paris every year to see and purchase the latest fashions. Charles was not yet married. Maybe they would meet at a party, and he would be captivated by her and her wardrobe. She had high hopes. And now this New York Jew was dashing them.

As I said, excommunication from the Church didn't bother her too much — after all, Charles wasn't a Catholic and she wasn't a believer, but marrying a member of a despised race — that was a different story. Many times, during our courtship, her mother would announce that if Anna persisted in this folly, she was going to jump off the balcony of their apartment to the street below. She would actually run towards the balcony to demonstrate her seriousness. Her husband or daughter always ran after her and prevented her from doing away with herself. No one actually believed she was going to commit suicide, but she was what is called today a 'drama queen' and repeated her performance before a standing audience many times over the course of the year. In the end her mother reconciled herself to the reality that Anna Maria probably wouldn't marry Prince Charles anyway, and I wasn't such a bad sort. She would never mention to anyone in her family that I was Jewish or that her daughter would convert. Not that they cared. With the exception of my future mother-in-law and people I didn't know in Mallorca, I never encountered any anti-Semitism in Spain.

In order to be officially excommunicated from the Church, Anna had to appear before her parish priest and explain why she didn't want to remain a Catholic. The priest also interviewed me so that he could determine that I wasn't a candidate for conversion. After the interviews there was a waiting period of a couple of months during which her name was posted on the doors of the parish church stating that she was an apostate and unless she repented would be excommunicated. She did not and thus was formally expelled from the Church. That was step one. Step two was finding an official who would marry us. The rabbi in Barcelona was not authorized by the government to perform conversions, so there could be no marriage in a Jewish ceremony. Anna's best friend, Pilar, had a good friend whom she met in university and was a recently defrocked priest. He had become an atheist but his standing as an official who could register a marriage had not yet been revoked. His family lived on a farm near the village of Santa Cristina de Oro. On their land was an abandoned church from the Middle Ages. He assured us that there were no crosses or other religious symbols in the building, and we agreed to have the ceremony there. The wedding vows were written by us, and he spoke very well and without any references to religion.

Chapter 19
Homecoming

After spending almost three years away from home I returned with my new wife to Rockville Centre. My parents graciously allowed us to stay with them until we could start working and afford to rent our own place.

Our first order of business was my wife's conversion. My parents had joined the Reform synagogue in town when my sister was old enough to go to Sunday school. As I mentioned earlier, the Conservative *shul* in town, which we belonged to when I was young, had a Hebrew school which met three times a week — from four p.m. to six p.m. twice during the school week and three hours on Sunday morning. My parents wanted my sister to be free for ballet and other culture enhancing classes during the week. The Reform Hebrew school was only three hours on Sunday morning.

Because of their membership, my wife did her conversion through the Central Synagogue. The rabbi was an old Polish Jew, who was born and raised in Warsaw before the First World War. His family had immigrated to the United States when he was a teen and he attended Hebrew Union College in Cincinnati, where he was ordained. He also had a PhD in Russian Literature and as a side job was a professor of that subject at a local college. He was in charge of conversions for the Hebrew Union College in New York City and had supervised my wife's conversion while we were still living in Spain. The conversion course consisted of her reading about twenty books on Judaism and writing a paper on why she wanted to be Jewish. After she read the books that my parents had sent from the States, I read them too. My wife got an 'A' on her paper. She was now qualified to convert.

For me, the incongruity of sitting with an old Polish Jew with a strong Eastern European accent, who was also a bareheaded 'rabbi', was a bit overwhelming. I had assumed that he had been brought up as an Orthodox Jew and had become an apostate. I was wrong. I asked him about himself and his personal beliefs. He told me that he was never educated in a yeshiva and his parents had been Reform Jews. He was also an atheist. I almost fell off my chair. When I asked him why he was a rabbi, he said he liked the counseling aspect of the job and belief in the *Aybishter* (G-d) was not a condition for ordination at HUC. He had only one picture in his office. It was of Albert Einstein. Albert, apparently, was his god.

The conversion was scheduled. When I asked him about a Jewish wedding, he answered, "*dina d'malchusa dina*" — the law of the land is the law. If we had been married in a secular ceremony, he couldn't perform a Jewish one. It was a *non-sequitur*. After all, how could he perform a marriage service for people who were already married? I didn't like his answer but didn't argue with him. The conversion service consisted of the Rabbi saying *Shema Yisrael* (Hear O'Israel the Lord is our Lord, the Lord is One) in front of the Ark and giving my wife the name Ruth (he told us that she had no choice in the matter, that every woman convert must be renamed 'Ruth' — which, as I learnt later, is false). He then gave her a certificate signed by himself and his secretary saying that Anna now had the added Hebrew name of Ruth, and she was officially a Jew. Neither my wife nor I felt that this was a valid conversion ceremony. Since we had read the books he assigned, we knew that halachically she needed some kind of an acceptance of *Mitzvohs* in front of a *Beis Din* of three observant men and *tevilah* (immersion) in a *mikveh* (ritual bath). Of course, we also knew that the Reform movement did not believe in *halacha*.

The next Shabbos we attended the Conservative synagogue in town, Temple Beth Shalom. As the youngest married attendees of the *shul*, we quickly made friends with the young rabbi and his wife. I remembered Rabbi Hillel Hyman from my attendance at the synagogue before my bar mitzvah. In those days he was a student at JTS, the Jewish Theological Seminary in New York — the Conservative movement's rabbinical training academy and he had a job reading the Torah at Beth Shalom on Saturday. He had a flair for dramatic reading that made the stories in the Torah come alive. When Rabbi Max Routtenberg had retired in 1972, the Board of the shul voted for Rabbi Hyman as his replacement. By that time, Hillel had been appointed an Assistant Professor of Talmud at JTS.

At the same time, we met another young couple, about seven or eight years older than us, both lawyers, who were *baalei teshuva* — Jews who came from secular backgrounds and became religious. They were both from Rockville Centre and, like me, had gone to Southside High School. They lived in a small apartment near the synagogue and had a couple of small children. They were also the NCSY leaders in Nassau County. NCSY or National Council of Synagogue Youth is a division of the Orthodox Union — the OU, whose symbol on thousands of food products allows American Jews who keep kosher to find kosher food at almost any supermarket in America.

Here's an interesting sidelight. Why is it that so many national brands have an OU symbol on the packaging when the number of Jews that keep kosher in the States is so small? Over thirty years ago I heard a lecture by the head of the Kashruth Division of the OU, Rabbi Berl Wein. He said that it was in the interest of food manufacturers to pay for kosher supervision because even though kosher Jews only numbered a few hundred thousand at that time, placement of product on a supermarket shelf is determined by market share of the product. The bestselling products are placed at eye level; the poorest sellers are on the bottom shelf. The competition among brands is fierce. If a product can gain even a half-percent in market share by making their product kosher, it was worth the cost.

As NCSY leaders this couple had a mob of high school kids at their house for Shabbos. Although they were observant, they lived in Rockville Centre, which did not have a religious Jewish community. On Friday nights, when there were usually no women attendees, the husband would *daven* (pray) at B'nai Shalom. On Shabbos morning he would walk for an hour to the Young Israel of Oceanside, an Orthodox *shul*. The Friday night meal was our first experience as a couple with a real Shabbos atmosphere. The food was delicious, there was singing and camaraderie. On Shabbos morning we often drove to B'nai Shalom to attend services and have lunch with the Hymans. Although he was a Conservative Rabbi, Hillel had grown up in an Orthodox home and attended the Young Israel of Hartford, Connecticut. He was a 'right-wing' Conservative, meaning that he kept the *halachos* of Shabbos and *kashrus,* etc. and resisted the innovations that were sweeping the Conservative movement at that time — like counting women in a *minyan* and calling a woman to the Torah. In fact, with the exception of Shabbos, the minyan he davened in at JTS had a *mechitzah,* a barrier separating the men from the women.

Hillel did not agree with the Reform rabbi in matters of marriage and conversion. He questioned my wife about matters of observance, including holidays and Shabbos and when he was convinced that she was sincere in her desire to become a part of the Jewish Nation, he convened a religious court, a *Beis Din* of three observant men, and she was taken to the *mikvah* in Far Rockaway for her *tevilah.* She now felt one hundred percent Jewish. Following that we had a *chuppah* (wedding canopy) in the *shul* and were married according to Jewish Law at least as interpreted by the Conservative Movement. My parents made a beautiful wedding reception for us at their home.

Hillel gave a Talmud class in the *shul* one or two evenings a week. We joined. It was my first exposure to *Gemara* (Talmud). We were encouraged to analyze the text and ask as many questions as we could think of. I was very inquisitive and by nature rarely agreed with any authority. Surprisingly, this was a virtue in learning Talmud. After a few months Hillel told me that I had a *'gemara kopf'* (a head for *gemara*), which I thought was a great compliment coming from a professor of Talmud. Of course, at this point I could barely read Hebrew and couldn't learn the text by myself, but I loved the classes and loved the intellectual stimulation of the ancient texts. I thought of becoming a Conservative Rabbi like Hillel. He told me that I would be accepted into JTS without a problem. But he urged me to think about that carefully, since, as we became more observant, we might want to move on to Orthodoxy. It was true. As I got more involved in the classes and reading and we were exposed more and more to the world of Orthodoxy through our friends at NCSY, I started thinking about going to Yeshiva University — an Orthodox institution and learning to be a rabbi there. There was one problem — my background. I didn't think they would accept me since I had no Hebrew skills. The *Gemara* is written in Aramaic and without punctuation or vowel points. I viewed my lack of skills as almost an insurmountable obstacle. At the same time, I had to think seriously about my future. I knew that rabbis weren't paid much, and it would probably take me at least another four years to be ordained during which time I wouldn't have time to work. I was also drawn to the legal profession and that seemed to offer a more realistic opportunity to make a living.

After we had been in the States for a month, we started looking for work. Living at home with my parents was fine, but as my mother used to say, "You can't have more than two adults under one roof." I got the hint.

Anna was hired by the Commercial Office of the Spanish Embassy, located in the Chrysler Building in Manhattan. She was to be their Public Relations representative. I got a job as a Title Examiner with the Title Guarantee and Trust Company in Mineola, the Nassau County seat. In those days, a title examiner spent his days in the basement of the County Records office researching the chain of title to a property and any liens or encumbrances thereon. I enjoyed my work. It was a bit like being a detective. If we had issued title insurance on the property in the past we needn't research the chain of title a second time, but only search for any liens, etc. from the date of our last examination. But, if we had never issued a policy before, we had to research the title back to as far as the records were available. Oftentimes this meant a hundred or a hundred and fifty years earlier. Property descriptions in a deed might read: "from the big rock on the Jericho Turnpike in the town of Old Westbury to the big tree stump on the north corner of the Murray farm, a distance of eighteen chains." I loved it. This was the stuff of history of my county. We also had to draw a map of the property. I could give expression to my more artistic side by drawing a most artful compass rose. Though most of the time the title search was short and there were few problems to make it interesting. I was very efficient and after about four months was promoted to 'Title Reader'. A 'reader' is the person who writes the title insurance policy. We didn't have to actually write the whole thing — that had been done by the legal department years ago. But the reader would examine the title examiner's report and write exclusions to the insurance. Any problem was automatically excluded. It seemed to me that this title business was a monumental con game. The buyer of a property, if he was getting a mortgage (which was 99.99% of the time), was required by the bank to purchase title insurance to protect their mortgage interest. If the buyer also wanted protection, he had to purchase a buyer's policy. The premium was a one-time fee. And to someone buying a house or condominium it was a relatively small percentage of the purchase price. Rarely, if ever, did anyone buying a house refuse to buy the insurance to cover his interest as well. After all, who wouldn't want insurance to guard against the possibility that he might have been swindled by a fraudulent seller, who wasn't the real owner? It was my job as a reader to see to it that no one would ever collect on a claim.

I suppose that there might have been some give and take if a sharp-eyed lawyer ever read the contract, but I don't recall ever getting resistance from a buyer's lawyer.

As a reader, I worked with our legal staff. We were taught some of the intricacies of property law. I was an eager student and the lawyers, who were mostly Jewish, encouraged me to go to law school. I didn't need much encouragement. I had no intention of spending my working life at a title insurance company.

I took the LSAT and applied to law schools. There were a few criteria that were very important to me. One was it had to be outside of the New York Metropolitan area. This was too bad because my mother worked in the Psychology Department of Hofstra University and was entitled to have her children attend its schools, including its Law School, tuition free. But I was tired of New York and New Yorkers and wanted a change of scenery. But I also loved my family and didn't want to live too far from them to visit often. We were becoming more religious and needed a warm Jewish community. Last, but not least, I needed to be near a city with an Alfa Romeo dealership and service center. Alfas were notoriously temperamental, and I was no mechanic. I needed an expert. On Long Island I had been incredibly lucky in this regard. A friend of mine from work had a friend who was a foreign car mechanic. She introduced me to Angel. Angel worked at a large dealership that sold Mercedes, Jaguars and Alfa Romeos. He was a Cuban immigrant and as an eighteen-year-old had participated in the Bay of Pigs invasion. I was fluent in Spanish, and we hit it off. Angel liked the other cars, but he fell madly in love with my Alfa, which was only one of six in the USA at the time. When I came to pick up my car, the first time I left it with him for a tune up, he showed me what he did. He opened the hood. The aluminum engine shone like a freshly minted silver coin. I was stunned. He explained that he had taken a toothbrush and cleaned off every spec of dirt or stain. Only then did he work on it. I had to force him to take payment for his work. He told me that he wanted nothing because it was a labor of love. I would never again find a mechanic for my Alfa who was remotely as dedicated or skilled as Angel.

I got into a number of law schools in different cities and my wife, and I took a week's vacation to explore the different communities that we might settle in. We researched the different Jewish communities and pitched our tent at campsites near the cities we investigated. We visited the law schools and scouted out the local community. We got to Cleveland, which was on the outskirts of the radius I had drawn on the map, on a Friday morning in July. Our friend, the NCSY director in Rockville Centre, had given me the phone number of his roommate from law school (he had gone to Ohio State). We were supposed to be staying with his friend's parents for Shabbos. When I called, he told me that he was sorry, but his mother was sick and they couldn't have guests, but he had arranged for us to stay with some friends of his. He gave me the address and we drove to Mike and Miki's house.

We were somewhat apprehensive. These people didn't know us, and they didn't even know our friend in New York. We were total strangers to them and, for all they knew, we could've been Bonnie and Clyde.

In Woodmere, New York, where we had moved a few weeks after finding employment we started keeping kosher and stopped driving on Shabbos. We attended Shabbos services at the Sons of Israel synagogue, a 'conservadox' shul (with a men's section, a women's section and a mixed section) and became friendly with the regulars there. We lived in Woodmere for a year. And as friendly as the congregants were at the services, we never received one invitation for a Shabbos meal.

Mike and Miki welcomed us with open arms. It was as if we were long lost relatives (which, in a way we were — as all Jews are one big family). We were so impressed with their hospitality that had we not met anyone else we probably would have moved to Cleveland Heights. But, after davening, in *shul* that Friday night almost everyone came over to me to introduce themselves and insisted that we must come to them for a meal. We weren't only treated like long lost relatives, but like long lost royal relatives. There were many young couples at the Young Israel and a number of them came around that Shabbos to Mike and Miki's to get to know us and offer any help they could. A month later, after deciding on Cleveland, we made another trip there to find a place to live. We didn't have to lift a finger. Other new friends found a large affordable apartment in the middle of the neighborhood for us. Invitations for Shabbos and Yom Tov came fast and furious. During the first three years that we lived in Cleveland there wasn't one Shabbos that we ate at home unless we chose to. The contrast to New York was profound. We had found our place.

Chapter 20
Choice of Profession

There are many reasons that people become lawyers. For me, the drama was the draw. There were a plethora of TV shows, movies and books about the lawyer as the defender of justice; the righter of wrongs; the white knight who saves his innocent client from the crushing jaws of prison; or of the government; or unscrupulous businessmen. This fit me. It was something like being Clark Kent — crusader for truth, justice and the American Way. I would settle for Clark and forgo Superman. I was quite argumentative as a teenager. I enjoyed taking the opposite position of anything anyone would say — whether I believed it or not — but especially if I believed it. (People who know me might think I haven't outgrown this, but I have, more or less.) Our family lawyer, my cousin Fred, had apparently noticed this in me and gave me books to read about being a lawyer. I remember 'My Life in Court' by Louis Nizer, one of the most famous trial lawyers in the country at the time., Also 'The Spirit of Liberty' containing the articles and speeches of Judge Learned Hand. It seemed to me to be the ideal profession for me — especially since I cringe at the sight of blood or even imagining an injury.

The summer after my sophomore year in college, I worked as a law clerk for Fred. After the Army in WWII, where he served in the signal corps, he went to Brooklyn

College and then Harvard Law School on the GI Bill. He was something of an idol in the family. I mean 'Haavad'! We didn't have too many Harvard men in the family. Obviously, Fred was quite academic and bright. He also was quite charming in a homespun, Lincolnesque way. And he was quite deliberate in his decision-making. He told me that before he graduated from Law School, he had studied different locations in the country on the cusp of major growth, where a small or sole practitioner might make his mark and decided on Bayshore in Suffolk County — way out on the Island. In those days, the phrase a 'struggling lawyer who hung out a shingle' was a common one and aptly applied to my cousin. Most lawyers were not the highly paid corporate, merger and acquisition guys. That came later when those lawyers became the stars of Wall Street and the legal profession. A large firm, even when I graduated from law school in 1976 was one hundred lawyers. In Fred's day they were much smaller and becoming a partner meant bringing in enough new paying clients that the firm would lose money if you were to take your business elsewhere or start your own firm. His practice started in his very modest 'home office' and gradually added clients as Bayshore and Suffolk County grew.

I don't remember many of the cases I worked on. They were fairly mundane. But two cases ignited my passion for the profession. Both were assignments from Legal Aid. The first was a murder. We drove out to Riverhead, the county seat, and met our client at the jailhouse. She was an 'exotic dancer' — at least that's what the local paper called her. She was white and about twenty-five years old, bleach blonde and quite tall. Originally from Detroit, where her father was a policeman, she had fallen off the straight and narrow and moved to New York where she took up with a Black drummer whose name was Johnny Berry. He cheated on her and she shot him dead. While her name wasn't Frankie, she absolutely reminded me of the song. For an eighteen-year-old kid from the staid NY suburbs this was a dream. I immediately empathized with her and her plight. Legally there wasn't much to do. She admitted the act and pled guilty to manslaughter and got ten years in prison.

The second case was different. It wasn't like a cheap paperback novel, or a Billie Holiday song. It was an outrageous travesty. Suffolk County, at the time, was still very rural. There were many farms, and the farmworkers were mostly illegal Mexicans or Central Americans. Our clients, three brothers, one a dishwasher and two farmworkers, were accused of the felony assault on three Suffolk County police officers — including one wheelchair bound retired policeman. They spoke no English. Fortunately for them and my cousin, I spoke Spanish. Suffolk County provided no interpreters at the time. I was allowed to interpret at their various court appearances.

They were scared. The story they told me inflamed my passion for justice. They were walking home down a county road one Sunday afternoon when a van pulled up beside them. Three or four drunken men, all off duty cops, jumped them and beat them badly. The retired wheelchair bound cop stayed in the van. Then they were arrested and taken down to the county jail, where, they told me, other policemen with rubber hoses beat them over a period of a few days. At their arraignment, my cousin asked for a doctor to examine them for bruises. Because they used rubber hoses it wasn't obvious how the bruises were inflicted. I was convinced of their innocence and decided that this is what I wanted to do — I would become a criminal lawyer and defend the oppressed and powerless. I don't remember what eventually happened to them. Most likely they also pled guilty to some lesser offense and were released on probation after a short jail sentence. Since Legal Aid cases paid almost nothing to the lawyer, it made more sense for my cousin to get a plea bargain from the prosecutor, than to spend weeks preparing for a trial.

That was not what I was going to do. I would fight every case up to the US Supreme Court, if necessary. Of course, at that time, I didn't have to think about paying a mortgage or supporting a family.

The first-year curriculum of Law School included a course in Criminal Law. I still had that dream. During that year I was stopped by the police in Cleveland Heights, Ohio for a speeding violation. From what I had learnt in class from Professor Lewis Katz, the universally acknowledged expert on Criminal Law in Ohio, and from my research into the legislative history of the law, I presented two very technical arguments as to why I wasn't guilty, even though I admitted to violating the posted speed limit. The judge decided in my favor. The next day, when I told Professor Katz about my case, he was dumbfounded. He told me that the judge that heard my case was notorious for always siding with the police. I told him my arguments and although he acknowledged their novelty and sound reasoning, he told me that they didn't really matter, and the judge must have liked me. I was at the same time both pleased with myself and a bit let down. But he congratulated me and told me that he himself had never beaten a speeding ticket in Cleveland Heights. I said: "I want you to know that I came to law school with the intention of becoming a criminal defense lawyer and your course has shown me that I could make it."

He answered, "Criminal Law is not a profession for a nice Jewish boy."

"Why not?" I asked.

"Because most criminal lawyers end up like their clients."

During my years of practice, I have seen a number of criminal lawyers in action. I have referred cases to them and, occasionally, co-counseled with them on cases involving my clients who were in bankruptcy proceedings. I have seen the sage advice of Professor Katz prove to be true in many cases but have also met lawyers who have resisted the pull to become legal accomplices to their clients. I'm not sorry that I followed his advice. Given my temperament and personality, I think I might have been unable to resist bending the law to win for my clients. However, that passion for justice for the downtrodden never left me. Occasionally, I had the good fortune to exercise it.

Chapter 21
Law School

At the end of August of 1973, I entered Case Western Reserve Law School. I hadn't been in school for four years and readjusting to the life of a student was a challenge.

I remember vividly the first day of Contracts class with Professor Arthur Austin. He asked us to raise our hands if we had a contract with the Law School. Almost no one did. I certainly didn't remember signing any paper that said 'Contract' on it. Then he stared down at the class list (there were about one hundred and twenty people in the class) and called out names.

"Mr Champion, do you have a contract with this law school?"

"No, I don't think so?"

"Mr Champion, what's a contract?"

"An agreement signed by two parties?"

"Ms Berringer, do you have a contract with this law school?"

"No."

"What's a contract?"

"A signed agreement between two parties?"

"Mr..."

I was deathly afraid that he was going to call on me and then I'd look like an idiot, because I realized that I didn't know what a contract was.

He then stopped the questioning and told us that a contract could be oral or written and it could be explicit or inferred. I felt like *Adom HaRishon* (Adam, the first man) after he ate from the forbidden fruit. My eyes were now open to the secrets of the law that most mortals weren't privy to.

This method of teaching is called the Socratic method and is used in most American law schools. It's radically different from the teaching method used in colleges, where the professor just drones on and on and if you're interested in listening that's good and if not, you fall asleep or in my case — doodle. From my notebooks in college, one might conclude that I was a very sloppy and untalented art student.

Because you could be called upon at any moment and be potentially embarrassed in front of one hundred and twenty students, one had to do the assigned reading and be alert. The Socratic method also helps students to come out of their shells and to feel confident about speaking in public and defending their position against a hostile questioner (in this case the professor). For me, it was the perfect school experience. While I was a good student in college and there were many classes that interested me, Law School and I were like two peas in a pod. I loved it. I did very well and was chosen to be a member of the Law Review for my second year and then was chosen to be an editor in my last year. Constitutional Law and Federal Jurisdiction were particular favorites of mine, and I also got a job as a student research assistant to my Constitutional Law Professor, Dr Ovid Lewis.

Professor Lewis was a Renaissance man. He was a genius

who apart from being a law professor and prolific legal writer had a PhD in Systems Analysis. He had been a professional violinist in a major symphony orchestra. And he was the Ohio Badminton Champion for the last ten years. He was a bundle of energy who would map out on the blackboard a flowchart showing the connecting the dots between various seemingly unrelated and diverse US Supreme Court cases. When I raved about his brilliance to a friend of mine who was learning in the Telshe Yeshiva, he asked if he could come with me to a class and see for himself. I got permission, and Aryeh sat in one of his classes and was astounded. Because of his narrow yeshiva education, he didn't think that *goyim* could be so brilliant. But it was obvious to him that Professor Lewis was a *gaon* — a genius.

While working for Professor Lewis, a former student, who was now a prominent criminal defense attorney in New Jersey, referred a case to him. He had represented Tony in a trial in the Federal Court of New Jersey. Tony was convicted of murder, extortion, racketeering and various other crimes. The proof came from FBI wiretaps. The defendant gave notice to appeal the conviction and Tony was granted bail. Professor Lewis was asked to represent the defendant on the appeal to the US Third Circuit Court of Appeals. He asked me to help him research and write the brief. We would be challenging the conviction based on violations of his Fourth and Fourteenth Amendment rights. If we could show that the wiretaps had been illegally obtained, then we had a good chance of having the whole case thrown out.

We received a transcript of the trial and all the materials garnered in the discovery phase of the proceeding. They included transcripts of the wiretaps. It made for fascinating reading. Our client was a 'made man' somewhat high up in the New Jersey mafia. His businesses were construction and garbage hauling. He built roads and other public works for the States of New Jersey and Delaware. He also had a monopoly on garbage hauling in a large part of northern New Jersey. The transcripts of the wiretaps revealed extortion of many subcontractors and threats to the lives of potential competitors and debtors and also of orders to eliminate the uncooperative. It was really damning stuff. This was our client. I felt very uncomfortable. Did I really want to represent a murderer and mafia chief? If we won, he would probably continue his criminal career and murder, extort and torture more people. Was this moral? I, of course, had been taught and believed that every person is entitled to representation by competent counsel and that if the wiretaps were illegally obtained, they would be 'fruits of the poisonous tree' and would be disallowed as evidence. But still, did I want to be involved?

A week after receiving the transcripts and the lower court's decision, we met the client. He came to the Law School. Tony was a big and heavy guy. With him was Rocco, a much bigger and heavier guy, who Tony referred to as his 'brother'. It was immediately apparent that Rocco had a big bulge under the left side of his suit. This was in the days before there were metal detectors at airports. We were sufficiently impressed.

Tony was very friendly and complained about the violation of his Constitutional rights. Rocco never said a word. Tony had heard great things about Professor Lewis from his former student and as a gesture of good will, in addition to the fee requested for the legal work, he was going to give to the Professor and to me Gold Double Eagle President watches, which cost about twenty thousand dollars each. This somehow assuaged my conscience and I started to feel something like outrage for the violation of constitutional rights by an oppressive government prosecution.

In the end, we wrote the brief and won the case. Tony never delivered the watches and I realized that maybe I had been wrong to dismiss my moral concerns.

In my third year of Law School, we had interviews for jobs. I was one of the top students in my class and got interviews with all the big firms in Cleveland. However, I had some major handicaps, like my *yarmulke* (skull cap), Shabbos, *Yom Tov* and *kashrus*.

In those days (the early seventies) in Cleveland it was uncommon to see a *yarmulke* in public and no one wore his *tzitzit* (fringes) out but tucked them inside his pants. Some of my friends wore a toupee in place of a *yarmulke* at work, but most didn't wear a head covering. And they had rabbinic authorities to rely on. *Frum* (religious) Jews wore hats outdoors. Although hats for men were going out of style, they were still common enough.

When I started law school, I had a dilemma. I didn't know if I should wear a *yarmulke* in school. On my first day I wore a woolen cap to my classes. I figured that since Blacks wore such hats indoors I could too and people might think that either I was a bit odd, or maybe I was showing solidarity with my Black brothers. For some reason or another, I was a bit embarrassed to be identified as a *frum* Jew. There were two other *frum* Jews in the school at the time. Neither of them wore a *yarmulke* or a hat. I decided I would do the same. And for the first few months I went to classes bareheaded. If I drank a coffee or bought a chocolate chip cookie (which happened to be from the kosher bakery in town), I would cover my head and make a *bracha* (a blessing) and then cover it again when it came time to make an after *bracha*. After a while I felt like a coward and a crypto-Jew and started wearing my woolen cap again.

At the start of my second year, one *frum* student, Yanky, started his first year. He wore a knitted *yarmulke*. He didn't seem to have a problem. I was embarrassed that I didn't have the courage to also wear a *yarmulke* and from that day onwards I did. To my surprise no one had anything to say about it. I then resolved not to let my fears of the reaction of others dictate my behavior.

In those days, large and middle size law firms were mostly segregated. There were WASP firms, Irish firms, Italian firms and Jewish firms. There were also a lot of small and sole practitioners of every ethnic group. In building a practice, lawyers, like insurance agents or accountants, develop social connections. They join golf clubs, social welfare organizations, political parties and churches and synagogues to make friends and build a reputation in the community. When someone in that community needs a lawyer, they hire someone they know and have confidence in.

Cleveland became a major industrial city in the late 1800's and major industrialists, including people like John D. Rockefeller were based in Cleveland. They needed lawyers and naturally hired those in their social orbit who developed the expertise their clients needed. It was only logical that the largest and oldest corporate firms in the city were composed mainly of WASPS. The Irish, Italians, Jews, Germans, Poles and other ethnic groups came to America later and only after establishing themselves in the middle class, sent their sons to professional schools, including law schools. When they started their businesses, they hired their friends and community leaders as their lawyers.

But times were changing. The Civil Rights Movement, Affirmative Action, the Equal Employment Opportunity Act, etc., all had a major effect on how businesses and law firms hired new associates. No longer could a firm decide not to hire a Black law graduate just because of his skin color or a Jew, just because he didn't fit into the firm's social culture or a woman because she was a woman. At the time I graduated, there were no Orthodox lawyers at any major firm in Cleveland and very few Jews. And those Jews that did practice with a large firm often had a close relative who was a major client of that firm. Even in New York, where there were hundreds of brilliant Orthodox lawyers, I wasn't aware of any Orthodox partners in a major Wall Street firm. And to my knowledge, there were no *yarmulke*-wearing lawyers at any major law firms in the United States.

Of course, law firms weren't going to change so fast. But they had to go through the motions of interviewing those whose academic standards qualified them to work in a top tier firm, even if they had no intention of hiring them. The year before I graduated one of the largest Jewish corporate firms in town sent a representative to the Law School to interview potential associates. Kevin O'Sullivan was one of the candidates. The interviewer asked him:

"Kevin, are you Jewish?"

"No sir," answered Kevin.

"I'm sorry Kevin, we only hire Jews."

Needless to say, that law firm was banned from recruiting on campus for the next three years. If the ban wasn't for discrimination by religion, it should have been for stupidity — I mean 'Kevin O'Sullivan'?

A friend of mine, Calvin Kay, a top graduate of the University of Michigan Law School, was being interviewed by Mr Smythe, a senior partner at one of the top WASP firms in Cleveland. Calvin was very athletic, tall, blond hair and blue eyed.

Mr Smythe told him that he too had graduated from Michigan Law School.

"It used to be a really great school, Calvin," he said.

"I think it's still pretty good Mr Smythe. Why don't you think it's not so good any more?"

"Too many damn Jews."

"Mr Smythe, I must tell you that I'm Jewish."

Mr Smythe could be forgiven for thinking that Calvin was not a Jewish name, that he didn't look like the stereotype of a Jew and, therefore, he could be frank. But he couldn't be forgiven for being an anti-Semite.

Cal told me that after that interview they had to give him the job or else face an embarrassing lawsuit. I think he was the first Jew they hired in their one-hundred-year history. He happened to be a brilliant lawyer and one of the top Estate Planning lawyers in the country. He eventually made partner despite the fact that he became Orthodox while at the firm.

I made up my mind that I was going to interview in a *yarmulke* and be upfront with my religious requirements. I had a number of close friends who worked as accountants or lawyers who were quite religious and wore toupees in place of a *yarmulke* and would eat fresh salads in *treif* (non-kosher) restaurants, when they had to eat with a client or with their firm, but I didn't want to compromise.

I had decided that if I couldn't get a job with my *yarmulke* I would go to Israel and study in yeshiva. This, laissez-faire attitude towards making a living was, no doubt, a result of having grown up in the sixties, when revolution was just around the corner, and also my mother's dictum of not working at a job that didn't make you happy. If I couldn't be myself, I couldn't be happy. My wife was fine with my decision. I really couldn't lose. I let Hashem make the decision.

I really loved the research and writing in Law School and my first choice of a job was to clerk for a US Supreme Court Justice. There one would be on the cutting edge of the law, especially constitutional law and from there a clerk would have his pick of any job he wanted — even with a *yarmulke* and Shabbos and Yom Tov. I sent my resume to all nine of them. But I was quite unrealistic. The Justices only hired those who had clerked for a Federal Appellate Court judge for at least a year. So, I applied to the US Appellate Court Judge whose office in Akron was closest to Cleveland.

Predictably, I was rejected by all the Supreme Court Justices, although I got very nice rejection letters signed by them. They all told me to reapply after a clerkship with a Federal Circuit Court Judge.

I got an interview with Judge Paul C. Weick of the US Sixth Circuit Court of Appeals. Despite the fact that I wore a *yarmulke* to the interview, I couldn't work on Saturdays, and had to leave work early on Fridays in the winter, he offered me the job after my interview. The Sixth Circuit met in Cincinnati every Friday, but he didn't think that it would be a problem for him if I left early on Friday afternoon. But, as a condition of the job he told me that I had to live in Akron. I turned him down. I wasn't willing to live in a place without an Orthodox religious community.

As I assumed, I got turned down by all the big corporate firms in Cleveland. Jones Day, for example, told me that all their associates were expected to be at work on Saturday mornings and they had to join the Shaker Heights Country Club and play golf and have lunch with clients at the club on Saturday afternoons. This was obviously a non-starter for me, but they went out of their way to tell me that they didn't discriminate against Jews and that they even had some Jewish associates at the firm.

One small corporate firm offered me a job. I would be the only Jew. All the partners and associates were WASPs with one exception — an Irish Catholic. They had broken away from a larger corporate firm, took a number of well-paying clients with them and were trying to build up their practice. The senior partner, for some reason, wanted me to hire me regardless of my conditions. He offered a salary at the level of the second largest corporate firm in Cleveland. He acceded to my requirements for Shabbos and Yom Tov. He even let me come to work later in the winter when sunrise was almost eight a.m. because I wanted to daven with a *minyan* and then go home and have breakfast. As it turned out, he was willing to put up with much more from me. A week before I was to start work, my father died. Now I needed to sit *shiva* (a seven-day mourning period) in New York and then I would need to say *Kaddish* for my father for eleven months. I also would have to let my beard and hair grow, etc. etc. When I told the senior partner, he had no problems whatsoever. But there was one serious problem that I was going to have, and I didn't think I had a palatable solution. In Cleveland in the winter, the sun sets before four p.m. I needed to *daven mincha* (afternoon service) with a *minyan* and say *Kaddish*. I told my boss that my options were to leave work at around three p.m. and come back at around five p.m. or I could try to organize a prayer meeting of ten men in my office, which would take about fifteen minutes at lunchtime. I thought this would sound like an insane idea to my boss, but I couldn't think of anything else. I probably would have preferred to lose the job than not to say *Kaddish* at the three daily prayer services.

My boss immediately agreed to the *minyan* in the office but added. "Why make it in your office? Make it in the conference room — it's so much larger." The Downtown Minyan in Cleveland started the day I started work. It is still going on today in the conference room of the office of one of my old partners almost fifty years later. It was obvious to me that this job was Heaven sent. As if to underscore that conclusion, Dave, the Irish Catholic associate, told me that he thought the senior partner was insane for choosing me, because the runner up for the job was a classmate of mine, who, while an average law student, was the son of the president of one of the largest banks in Cleveland. The bank president not only was a very prominent citizen of Cleveland, but he had also promised the senior partner the bank's business if he hired his son. Obviously, G-d's hand was directing my future.

As a concession to my boss and to show him how reasonable I was, I told him that although I preferred to wear my *yarmulke* all the time, if there was any situation in which he would feel uncomfortable with my badge of Jewishness, he should tell me. I would take it off to meet with those clients. He told me that he didn't think it would be a problem with anyone except two clients — both manufacturers. In his opinion, he told me quite frankly, they were anti-Semites. I didn't know his definition of an anti-Semite, but his ethnicity was German and before I started working, he invited my wife and I to his house for a reception. He got drunk and joked about the Holocaust and about Jews being made into soap that his relatives used. I could only imagine what our anti-Semitic clients were like.

Chapter 22
Mother's Illness

During the spring of my second year of law school, the week before final exams, my father called with tragic news. My mother was in Long Island Jewish Hospital on the North Shore of Long Island in critical condition. While at a Broadway show in the city with another couple, she was stricken with a terrible headache. They left the theater immediately and as they were driving back home on the Northern State Parkway, she lost consciousness. New Hyde Park was close by, and they drove to the emergency entrance of the hospital. Doctors quickly determined that she had a brain aneurysm. The prognosis was poor. It was late that night when my wife and I set out on the eight-hour drive to New York.

My mother was young and beautiful. She was only forty-seven and had always been in excellent health. She was a few weeks short of twenty years old when I was born and as a teenager, most people thought we were brother and sister. She loved that. She was trim and exercised regularly. During the previous year she started having severe headaches. Her doctor didn't attribute them to anything more than normal stress. And there was plenty of that.

My father's cancer, after six years of remission, had returned more aggressively than before. A year or so before, his landlord had tripled the rent on his store and drove him out of business. Creditors were hounding him and my mother — calling the house constantly, disturbing their tranquility and putting them under terrible stress. He retrained as an insurance agent and financial advisor, having to study for the licensing exams in his fifties. He was just starting to build a clientele and was struggling to try to make ends meet. In addition to completing her Master's Degree in Psychology and her job as an administrator at Hofstra University's Psychology Department, my mother started organizing Sunday yard sales throughout the county to help earn extra money. So, there was plenty of stress. But what happened was totally unexpected — as aneurysms are.

Once at the hospital I had endless questions for the neurosurgeon about her condition. He explained that most aneurysms are congenital, and it was like a ticking time bomb. After forty-seven years, five months and twelve days it exploded. He drew a diagram that looked like a tire blowout. An aneurysm occurs when an artery has a weakness in its outer wall. The pressure of the blood flow can cause the artery to balloon out of its outer sheath and when it ruptures, blood gushes out. Blood in the brain damages and kills brain cells, which depending on where bleeding occurs, will often lead to death unless the vessel heals itself or is repaired by surgery. When I first arrived, my mother was very weak, but conscious and fully aware of her condition. We spoke for an hour or so about Jewish immigration to the United States — the topic of her senior year American Studies thesis. I called the Dean of the Law School and told him what happened. He was very solicitous and wished my mother a speedy recovery and told me not to worry about my finals. We'd work something out.

Over the next few days my mother's condition worsened.

She lost consciousness again and the doctors attributed it to a fresh bleed. They told us that to operate before the bleeding stopped would be almost a certain death sentence. After another couple of days passed and no cessation of bleeding, I asked the neurosurgeon what were the odds of her surviving an operation while she bled. He told me that he would give her a twenty-five percent chance of survival, but if we did nothing there was almost a one hundred percent chance of her dying within the week. And even if she did survive the operation, he had no way of knowing what her quality of life would be.

We didn't know what to do — to let her die or to try to save her. And even if she lived, what kind of a life would she have? Maybe she'd be in a vegetative state for years after that until the end of her life? Is there a value to that kind of life? Would she be better off if we did nothing and let her die? I called friends of mine in the religious community in New York for guidance. Someone suggested that I ask the Lubavitcher Rebbe, a man known for his sage advice. I called the Rebbe's secretary and asked the question. When I called back for the answer, I was told that the Rebbe said we should do the operation.

The operation took all day. We were all in and out of the waiting room pacing the halls and very anxious. That evening the doctor came out of the operating room and told us that because my mother's heart was very strong, she didn't die on the table. He stopped the bleeding and repaired the artery. Most likely she would be in a coma for a period of time, how long he couldn't guess, and then, when and if she came out of the coma, we'd see what damage had been done.

My wife and I stayed in New York for a few more weeks while my mother was in a serious but stable condition in the

ICU unit at the hospital. After that we returned to Cleveland. It was now summertime. I visited the Law School and met with the Assistant Dean. He told me that he had polled all my professors for that second semester had they all agreed to give me a pass for my courses. The pass wouldn't interfere with my place in the class (I was seventh — which I interpreted as a reward from Hashem for keeping the Shabbos day) or my grade point average. I have always felt a real debt of gratitude to the Law School for their understanding during a particularly difficult period of my life.

My mother was in a coma in the Intensive Care Unit for the next six months. Because of her excellent health insurance policy from Hofstra, she was able to stay until then, but after exhausting the $1.5 million limit of the policy she had to move elsewhere. There was no more insurance, and our family had no money. She qualified for Medicaid and was moved to a state convalescent hospital in Rockland County, about a two-hour drive from Rockville Centre.

For the next year, my father drove every morning and evening to the hospital to be at her bedside. In between he worked as an insurance agent. Even for a person in good health that would have been a punishing schedule, but for someone who had cancer, it hastened his decline. He was literally running himself ragged and getting almost no sleep. He died within that year, at fifty-seven.

My mother was hospitalized for the next twenty-three years and finally died at the age of seventy of a staph infection in a nursing home in Babylon. She 'regained' consciousness after two years but was left blind and paralyzed on one side of her body. She had spotty recollections of her childhood but didn't remember that she was married or had children. The radio next to her bed was always tuned to a 'golden oldie' station. She would sing along to every song. The one thing she never forgot was the tune and lyrics to every song she ever heard.

I often wondered if we made the right decision by choosing to operate. Being an optimist, I thought she was fortunate not to be conscious of her condition. She was almost always in good spirits, except when she felt pain. In that state she was a total *onais* — she had no responsibility for any of her actions or speech. While some people earn their *Olom Haba* (the World to Come) by keeping *mitzvohs* and avoiding *aveiros* (sins), how can those who are incapable of thinking or action earn their *Olom Haba*? If Hashem put a person on this earth, who at birth was in that condition, or fell into that condition later in life, there must be a reason. It couldn't be that she was doomed to be devoid of *zechuos* (merits) in the World to Come. Her suffering in this world and the non-performance of *aveiros* must bring merit to her soul. My mother lived for twenty-three years as a perfect *tzaddekas* (righteous person). I concluded that her portion in the World to Come must be very great.

Chapter 23
New Beginnings

Although I was going to be working for a corporate law firm, my boss was willing to let me continue working on a *pro bono* case I had begun a few months before. My very good friend, Sam, was working as an accountant for a large accounting firm in Cleveland. He had finished his course work for his Master's Degree in Accounting at a local state university and had passed all his CPA exams. But there was a snag. The school required a certain grade point average in order to receive the degree. He had failed a course. And although he had enough credits to graduate, his GPA was not sufficient. His job required a degree in accounting. Since his undergraduate degree was in chemistry, he needed the Master's Degree in Accounting to keep his job.

According to the student handbook issued when he entered the school, his GPA was sufficient for the degree, but the school had changed the rules for computing a GPA while he was in his last year of the course. He was married with a young son and worked full time. He didn't want to have to take another class at night and miss staying home with his family after a long day's work. He asked me if I could think of some way to help. I remembered that first day of Contracts with Professor Austin and knew that Sam had a contract with the university and that the handbook contained many of the provisions of that contract. Since Sam never agreed to any changes in the terms, the prior handbook still applied to him and, therefore, he was entitled to a degree without any further coursework. Because the school was an agency of the State of Ohio it was not only in breach of its contract with him, but also was violating his Fourteenth Amendment rights under the US Constitution. The day after I got notice from the Supreme Court of Ohio that I had passed the bar exam and could now practice law, I filed his complaint in the Federal Court for the Northern District of Ohio.

The following day my boss called me into his office and asked me if I had read the Plain Dealer that day. I hadn't.

He spread open his copy and on page two was a sizable article about the federal case filed against Cleveland State University the day before by Attorney William Semenov. I was very surprised. I never spoke to the papers about the case and the only people who knew about it were Sam's family, my secretary who typed it, and my boss. It never occurred to me that the local paper had reporters who check the daily docket of the courts.

I was contacted by the head litigation partner of Squires, Sanders and Dempsey, one of the largest firms in town. He read my fifteen-page complaint and although he told me that it was totally without merit and would fight it with the considerable resources of the State of Ohio, he was willing to talk settlement with me, in order to avoid costly and unnecessary litigation. I had hoped to make history with this case, and no one makes history with a settlement, but I had an obligation to my client. Sam's interest in legal history was not the same as mine. He just wanted a degree. I asked Squire's lawyer what he proposed. They would allow Sam, at no cost to himself, to take an independent studies course with an accounting professor of his choice. If he passed the course, Sam would get his degree. This was obviously a face-saving move on their part.

I suppose I could have held out for attorney fees, but since I had a well-paying job, the money wasn't very important to me. Sam and I had a good friend who was a professor in the accounting department at Cleveland State. He agreed to supervise the course and a deal was struck. Sam got an 'A' in the course and his degree. That pretty much ended my career as a constitutional lawyer.

During those first years of practice at the firm I had a major victory — although it wasn't in the courtroom. One of our clients, the Catholic Cemeteries Association of the Diocese of Cleveland, called our attention to a spate of vandalism at local cemeteries. It seemed that teenagers were getting drunk, entering graveyards and knocking down monuments and headstones. The repairs were quite costly and there was no one to collect from. Violators were not being caught. And there was little law enforcement could do to prevent recurrences.

The newspapers mentioned that cemetery vandalism was only a misdemeanor in Ohio, so that even if caught, the perpetrators would only get a 'slap on the wrist'. My boss, who was very creative, thought that the way to remedy this situation was to upgrade the crime of cemetery vandalism to a felony. And he assigned me that task of working with Father Clines, the director of the Cemetery Association along with other attorneys who represented other cemetery associations in the State. There was a certain poetic nature to the enterprise. Here we were, two 'men of the cloth' — he with his collar and me with my *yarmulke* fighting the pagan vandals.

My task was to draft legislation changing the penalty to a felony and to write a brief in support, which I would then present to all the members of the Ohio State Legislature. Using the tools I learnt in Law School, I spent a few weeks at the Cuyahoga County Law Library, researching and drafting the legislation and writing a fifty-page brief comparing Ohio's penalty for cemetery vandalism to those of other States. Ohio was one of very few States in the Union to treat that crime so lightly. Almost all the others made it a felony. I compared it to flag desecration, which was a felony in Ohio. One was an affront to a symbol of the country, the other a personal attack on the family of the deceased and to the norms of a society, which honored it's dead. I made an argument that the emotional injury for cemetery desecration was at least as great as for flag desecration and probably greater since it was also personal. The brief was full of hyperbole and outrage. Father Clines loved it and put me in touch with a lawyer in Columbus who represented an umbrella group of Catholic cemetery associations in Ohio. He had connections to politicians in the Legislature and arranged for sponsors for the bill. As its author, I was invited to testify in front of the Judiciary committee. It was quite a new experience for me, and I enjoyed it. In the end, the bill passed eighty-nine to nil. Apparently, the vandals had few lobbyists and, if they did, they didn't do a very good job. My boss was very proud of me and told me that I would remember that victory for the rest of my life. He was right. Almost fifty years later, I still do.

I had been doing estate planning for a wealthy manufacturer whose company we represented. I had never met Mr Schultz, the client but, of course, knew a lot about him and his family. He was our wealthiest client and one of those that my boss considered an anti-Semite. His children had German names, like Franz, Helmut and Heidi. They spoke German and since childhood had spent their summers in the Bavarian Alps. They all were married to Germans. It was a given that Mr Shultz had been a Nazi Party sympathizer and had probably donated large sums to the Party in the thirties.

The annual meeting of the Board of Directors of his company, which manufactured parts for nuclear reactors, was to be held at the company's offices at noontime. I was appointed the assistant secretary of the company, and my job was to take notes and write them up as minutes of the meeting, as required by Ohio law. It was the summertime, so *mincha* was quite late in the afternoon and there was no problem getting to a *minyan* and saying *Kaddish*. On the other hand, it was to be a lunch meeting. I wasn't sure how I was to handle it. My solution was to take one almond (*bracha haetz*), a small piece of celery (*bracha adamah*) and a Pringle (*bracha shehakol*) keep them in a small plastic bag in my pocket, excuse myself for a moment, leave the boardroom, find a hidden nook somewhere between the boardroom and the men's room, put on my *yarmulke,* make the *brachos* and eat the food in my bag and then uncover my head and go back into the boardroom and eat a salad. I could make an after *bracha* when the meeting was finished and was back in the car with my boss.

Salad was served. But there was meat in the salad bowl and a dressing whose ingredients I could not discern. I passed. Next was a soup. I wasn't going to eat food cooked in *treif* pots. I told the server that I didn't want the soup. When they served the pork chops and I passed again, Mr Shultz noticed that I wasn't eating — only drinking water. He asked me why I wasn't eating? I was afraid that his next question would be, "Are you by any chance a Jude?" at which point I would be taken away by some plain clothes SS men and tortured in a special chamber in the factory basement.

I answered, "I have a fever and a stomach flu. I'm not hungry and I can't hold down any food."

Mr Shultz, his *rachmonos* (pity) stirred, asked his secretary to bring me tea and toast.

I said yes to the tea but told him that I couldn't eat the toast. (Maybe they would smear it with lard to test me).

Shultz never suspected a thing. Or if he did, he played it cool.

I spent two years at the firm. During my last year, the fortunes of the firm were declining. We had lost some of the better clients and had hired my classmate whose father was the bank president. It helped for a while, but eventually the firm let me go and eventually merged with a larger firm.

I was now unemployed and in no hurry to get another job. I needed a vacation. I had six months of unemployment payments, which paid me a living wage. The only drawback was that I was required to look for work in my profession and report every week to the unemployment office with proof that I had had at least two interviews for jobs in that time. I received a little book in which potential employers attested that they had met with me. That wasn't so hard. I applied to all the major law firms in Cleveland, but never encountered a partner, like my old boss, who was as inspired to take me on with all my *mishagassin* (quirks).

Now that I had some time on my hands, our friend, Sam's

accounting professor, asked me to help him get tenure. It was publish, or perish, for him and he was having a hard time writing. With his collaboration, I wrote two peer reviewed articles on tax related subjects that we published in professional journals. He got tenure and I got a *mitzvah*.

Chapter 24
My Short-Lived Career as a Real Estate Mogul

While I was working at the corporate firm, Dave, one of my friends in the Jewish community, convinced me and seven other friends to invest in real estate. The plan was to buy a run down three-storey house in East Cleveland, a predominantly Black suburb adjacent to Cleveland Heights, fix it up and rent out its three apartments to families. We hoped to get those who were qualified to receive Section 8 housing subsidies. The advantage of Section 8 is that the landlord receives up to two thirds of the rent directly from the US Government. We each chipped in a relatively small amount of money, I think it was $2500, and bought the house for cash. Dave's father, Harry, was a contractor and promised to give us a good deal on the repairs and, in addition, because of his son's involvement, he would provide management for free. We would reinvest the profits from the rental income and buy more houses, fix them up and rent them out, and eventually sell the houses at a huge profit and buy apartment buildings and hotels. I could already see myself as Mr Monopoly with a top hat. I already had the mustache.

Things began to go wrong almost immediately. The cost of repairs was underestimated. Instead of being limited to our original investment, we had to add an additional investment of $2500. The speed of the project was also miscalculated.

Instead of it taking three months to complete, as we were promised, it took eight months. It seems that Harry was completing other jobs first and didn't have the manpower to work on our project.

As time went on, I met Brad, another investor who was pursuing a similar plan down the street from our property. Although Brad was also only in his late twenties, he had been doing this full time for years and without partners. He had his own crew. He told me that our contractor did not have a sterling reputation and we should monitor the construction charges. He also told me that we overpaid for the property and that it was likely our contractor pocketed a tidy sum from the owner on the sale. And, unless we had a manager without a conflict of interest, we would lose money.

His words proved to be prophetic.

Although we were eight partners, only Yanky and I were willing to take responsibility for managing the property. We were still using Harry as our contractor, but now we were watching the expenses. The only problem was that neither of us knew anything about the costs of building or repairs. When the house was finished in late August, we put ads in the local paper and quickly found three seemingly qualified tenants to occupy the three apartments. Our responsibilities, as the landlord, included making repairs and furnishing heat, electricity and water to the units. The tenants promised to pay their portion of the rent, the balance coming from the US Department of Housing and Urban Development under Section 8. At long last we were in business. Or so we thought.

When October rolled around and the second month's rent came due, we encountered our first difficulty. Only one tenant had the money for that month's rent. Repeated visits to the other tenants, met with excuse after excuse. Since neither of us was in the business of collecting debts, we weren't very good at it and kept buying the excuses made. We also discovered another troubling fact. As we well knew, in Cleveland, beginning in October, the weather often gets quite cold. By November or December, the temperatures could fall to the low single digits Fahrenheit. Both Yanky and I kept our thermostats at about sixty-eight degrees, which was comfortable if you wore a light sweater. Our tenants liked to dress in shorts and tee shirts and kept the thermostat at ninety-five degrees. Stepping into their apartments was like stepping into the tropical rain forests of Africa. The gas bill for heating was astronomical and we had to pay it.

It also turned out that Harry was not a very good contractor and things kept breaking. I bought a book on home repairs and Yanky, and I put on our jeans and work shirts after coming home from a hard day at the office and went to the property to fix the broken plumbing or the falling plaster. Neither of us was very handy and the quality of our workmanship left something to be desired. But we had no money to pay professionals, so we were the default plumbers, electricians and carpenters. My dreams of the life of a successful real estate investor soon dissolved into thin air.

The final nail in the coffin, to use an acquired carpenter's phrase, was when we were sued by one of our tenants for a huge amount of money. I think it was in the neighborhood of $200,000. She alleged that because of our shoddy workmanship, a large piece of plaster from the bathroom ceiling fell on her back and caused serious and permanent injury and damage.

She claimed that she had been a nightclub singer before the accident, but as a result of our negligence and the resulting injury, she couldn't hit the high notes any more. Worse still, this was a permanent condition. Her voice would never come back. We had 'broken' her voice and now she had no means of support. And, as absurd as it seems, she also claimed that as a direct result of the falling plaster she became pregnant and now would have to care for a child. She demanded that we pay for the future hospital bill for the baby's delivery and the costs of raising the child until it reached its majority at age eighteen. As hard as it was for us to believe, she even found a lawyer to file her ridiculously absurd and frivolous lawsuit.

We had insurance that covered litigation and, of course, both of us were qualified lawyers working for corporate firms. We knew a nuisance suit when we saw one. We wanted to see justice done and did not want to settle with the plaintiff. The lawyer from the insurance company thought otherwise and after extensive pleadings and discovery settled the case. We were very disappointed.

We told the other inactive partners that we were finished with the real estate business, and we should look for a buyer. We finally sold the house to Brad at a significant loss, but at least we had a tax write off and a valuable life's lesson: "Don't invest your hard-earned money into a business unless you know what you're doing." As a wise man once told me. "It's easy to make money. The hard part is keeping it." We found that making the money was also hard.

Chapter 25
On My Own

As the six months of unemployment benefits ended, I started thinking about opening my own practice. Aryeh, my friend whom I had taken to Professor Lewis' class, and now a Rabbi in Canton, Ohio, told me that one of his congregants, Gary Kraft, was a lawyer who, with his wife and young family, had recently become observant. Since there was no Orthodox community or religious school in Canton, he was looking to move to Cleveland. Gary was a sole practitioner with a burgeoning bankruptcy practice and was looking to partner with someone in Cleveland, so that after a couple of years he could wind down his practice in Canton and have a practice in Cleveland that could afford him and his family a decent living.

I knew almost nothing about Bankruptcy Law. It's a specialty that in those years only a few firms practiced. If a corporate firm represented a business that needed restructuring, they would refer it out to a bankruptcy firm. If an individual needed to file bankruptcy, he would go to a bankruptcy lawyer. The Bankruptcy bar in Cleveland was almost all Jewish. I had taken a course in Bankruptcy Law in Law School, but it was heavy on procedure and light on substance. Like most lawyers I was aware that if a person was in financially dire straits, he could file a Chapter 7 and if a business wanted to try to save itself from collapse and restructure its debt, it could file a Chapter 11. That was basically all I knew.

I drove down to Canton, to meet Gary at his office and he gave me a lecture about bankruptcy law and its different relevant chapters. Here's a short synopsis of the U.S. Bankruptcy Law.

In England of the seventeenth and eighteenth centuries, where our American legal system was born, if a person owed money to another and couldn't pay, his assets — all that he owned — would be seized by the Sheriff (like the Sheriff of Nottingham) for the benefit of his creditors. His property was sold at public auction and the proceeds distributed to the creditors to pay off his debts. If the debtor didn't have enough assets to cover his debts (which he almost never did) he was thrown into debtors' prison, where he would languish in hunger, squalor and disease until he died, unless some family member managed to scrape up enough money to pay off his debts and free him (or unless Robin Hood freed him, and he became one of the Merry Men living in Nottingham Forest). Without a breadwinner, his family suffered along with him.

Surprisingly enough, this system still exists today in one form or another in most countries of the world. Even in a country as 'enlightened' as Israel, which was founded by socialists, debtors are never free from their debt. If one owes money, all his assets are taken away and sold for the benefit of creditors. If he has a job, most of his wages are garnished and paid to the creditors. If he doesn't pay, he will be in contempt of court and thrown into prison. There is no relief. Once adjudicated a bankrupt, his earnings for the next five years are seized by the court and given to his creditors. It is very common in Israel for people who owe a lot of money to leave the country on a false passport (since creditors can easily obtain a court order to prevent a debtor from exiting the country). Using a false identity, he establishes residency in another country and can never return. In Brooklyn I have occasionally bumped into neighbors who ran away from Israel because of debt. I have also known debtors here in Israel to live 'underground', i.e., to move away from their registered address and avoid all contact with the State, so that they can survive on their undeclared income. The reason for this state of affairs has mostly to do with Israel's banks. At the beginning of the State only political parties were able to get bank charters. The largest bank was and is Bank HaPoalim — the Workers Party bank. Banks don't like to lose money, and the Socialist Workers party bank was no exception. It was able to get the Knesset (parliament) to pass legislation making it impossible to receive a 'fresh start'. The problem in Israel was compounded by the fact that banks would almost never give a mortgage without two co-signers. Since almost everyone needed a mortgage, almost everyone was also a co-signer. In those cases where the borrower couldn't pay his mortgage, for whatever reason, the banks would collect from the co-signer who never even got the benefit of the money lent, pushing him into the poorhouse.

It is interesting to note that whole countries were founded by debtors. Australia is the best example. It was originally a penal colony for England. And most of its convict-colonizers were debtors or poor people arrested for stealing food to feed their families.

While we learn in school that the American Colonies were havens for the religiously persecuted, and that is undoubtedly true, many, if not most of the early colonists were either debtors or convicts who had been imprisoned for petty theft and were given or took the opportunity for a fresh start in a new land. The Founding Fathers embedded in the Constitution a new concept that abolished the idea of debtors languishing in prison until his relatives repaid the money he owed and allowed that person who couldn't afford to pay off his debts to declare bankruptcy, surrender his property and receive a discharge of all debts no matter how great they were. He could then start all over again without the weighty millstone of debt around his neck. In fact, I would conjecture that the financial success of America could be attributed to its bankruptcy laws. It encourages businessmen to take risks they wouldn't otherwise take. If they fail, they can dust themselves off and start over again. The most current example of this is Donald J. Trump, whose businesses have failed over and over again, but was rescued by the bankruptcy law until he eventually achieved financial success. (Although maybe America would have been better off had he languished in debtor's prison).

In addition, each state has laws that allow debtors to keep certain property exempt from seizure by creditors. In some states, like Texas, there is a homestead exemption that shields all the equity in one's principal residence from creditors. Many other states are less generous in their homestead exemptions, but they all have them. Other assets, such as automobiles, tools of the trade for a workman, clothing, retirement accounts, certain cash in the bank, etc. are often exempted.

The idea of a discharge of debts and a fresh start and exemptions of certain assets from seizure by creditors didn't originate in America. In fact, the earliest mention of a discharge of debts is mentioned in the Torah.

"At the end of every seven years, you shall celebrate the *shemitah* (the sabbatical year). And this is the *shemitah;* release everyone who owes you money; do not dun your friend and brother (for his debt) because it is called a *shemitah* (a release) to Hashem." (Deuteronomy 15:1-2)

It's quite amazing to me that thousands of years ago the Torah declared a discharge of all debts every seven years. To my knowledge, there has never been a country or society on earth that has shown such compassion or sensitivity to debtors as G-d required of the Jewish People. From the earliest records of the Greeks and Romans, selling debtors and their wives and children into slavery for non-payment of debt was normal.

As to exemptions for debtor's property, the Mishnah in *Arachin* 6:3, mentions food, clothing, household furnishings and tools of the trade as exempt from seizure by the Temple's treasurer if one pledged money or property and couldn't pay.

"Although someone who pledged (to the Temple) may have their property seized, they must be left with enough food for thirty days, clothing for two years, bed and bedding, shoes and tefillin… If he is a workman, we give him two work tools of each kind…"

The Founding Fathers, who were enlightened men of solid religious education (many of them read and understood Hebrew) incorporated those ideas gleaned from the Torah into the guiding document of our new country.

The procedure I mentioned above is what is known as Chapter 7 or simply, 'bankruptcy". But there are other provisions in the Bankruptcy Law, which allow for a debtor to keep all of his property and repay all or a portion of his debt, without interest, over a long period of time. These are known as Reorganizations or Restructuring of debt. The most well-known of them, is Chapter 11, in which a corporation voluntarily submits a plan to pay off its creditors while continuing to operate. The creditors have meetings and vote to approve or reject a plan and may negotiate with the debtor to amend the plan. There is another Reorganization chapter, which applies to individuals. That is Chapter 13. And Gary Kraft was the king of Chapter 13 filings in Northern Ohio.

I was intrigued by the concept. Here was a way to protect debtors from rapacious creditors and, at the same time, restore the pride and honor of the debtor by actually repaying the debt. I remembered how, when my father's business was failing and he was dying of cancer, creditors hounded him day and night.

This form of practice greatly appealed to me because I wasn't helping a business or a well-to-do person to negotiate the ins and outs of estate tax or the income tax code, or even to lock up some poor misdirected teenagers, but I was a kind of a Superman, or Clark Kent — protecting the poor and weak from the dripping fangs of the rich and strong.

Gary came to Cleveland to see what the competition was like. There wasn't any. There were almost no Chapter 13 filings in the Federal Court in Cleveland. We met with the Chapter 13 Trustee, Myron Wasserman, a Federal Court appointee, who administered the few cases that were filed. Gary told him that he had to be prepared for a great influx of work and that he would put him in contact with a former Chapter 13 trustee in Oklahoma City who now had a business which assisted Chapter 13 trustees around the country to administer their cases. He had a large computer that could handle a huge number of cases. He would issue checks to attorneys and creditors and generate court orders to employers to deduct the agreed upon amount from the debtor's paycheck to fund the plan. Myron agreed to meet with the computer guy and soon afterwards automated the administration of the cases.

I agreed to open an office in Cleveland with the name Kraft and Semenov and traveled down to Canton every day for a week and learnt how to compose a plan for repayment and the court procedures.

I rented an office and hired a secretary — a young, smart, Bais Yaacov (an orthodox Jewish high school) graduate who could type. Giti would field the incoming calls, sit with the clients before I met with them and sort out the various bills and demand letters they brought to the interview, and organize the information on Gary's forms.

The first thing I would tell the client was, "From now on you are to tell every creditor that calls…'Speak to my attorney, Mr Semenov' and hang up." It was illegal for creditors to call a debtor after being informed that he was represented by counsel. This usually resulted in a broad smile. I began the interview by verifying the information and determining if there was enough income after household expenses to fund a Chapter 13 plan. If there was, I'd explain to the client the difference between a Chapter 7 and a 13. Inevitably clients chose Chapter 13. There were a number of reasons for this. One was that most debtors, at least the ones in Northern Ohio, really wanted to pay their creditors back. They had incurred the expense on their credit cards or on an installment plan with a furniture or appliance store and wanted to pay the creditor what they owed. Very few people were interested in being a 'dead beat', in their own eyes. If they owned a home and were behind on mortgage payments, a 13 could stop a foreclosure and restructure the amount in default and pay it out over a long period of time.

I would craft a plan suited to each debtor, and in almost all cases we were able to save their homes and cars and every other possession of value. When they told me they had no money to pay me, I would tell them that was no problem, I would be paid through the court. Part of the money coming out of their paycheck would go to pay me. The only money they needed was sixty dollars to start the case — and even that could be paid through the court's payroll deduction. The relief felt by the debtor after that initial meeting was palpable. Frowns and depressive looks, dissipated. Smiles and confidence returned. Almost everyone felt that a great weight had been lifted from their shoulders.

From maybe one of two filings a month in the Federal Courthouse in Cleveland before I started the practice, we were soon doing thirty to forty cases. I was very popular with the creditors' attorneys because, as Gary had discovered, most debtors acknowledged their debts and wanted to pay them back in full, if given the opportunity. This full payment was without interest or penalties, which very often, amounted to more than the underlying debt. The business grew and generated other legal business particularly Workman's Compensation and personal injury cases. We eventually hired other attorneys to help us with the non-bankruptcy business, one of whom later became our partner, Larry Ehrenthal. After about two years, Gary moved to Cleveland and was now in the office almost every day.

I soon realized what a bonanza the bankruptcy practice was. It was impervious to economic cycles. When times were good and people were employed, they would spend without thinking much about how they were going to pay the money back. In Cleveland, with a huge industrial base, auto plants and steel mills and tool shops paid their unionized workers well, and if they needed more money, they could always work overtime at time and a half. They had enough to make the payments. The problems came when there was a hitch in the economy or in their personal lives. In times of recession or downturns in business, a worker might get laid off or have his hours reduced and now didn't have enough to make timely payments. Or there might be a health crisis in the family, or some other major unforeseen expense that crippled their ability to pay their other debts. They would then fall into arrears on their credit card debt, their car payments, or their mortgage payments. Creditors and collection agencies would harass them. Repo men would seize their cars and boats. This situation could last for a year or two with the debtor making some payments to keep his creditors at bay. But eventually the debt would overwhelm the debtor and he would have to seek help. It often happened that by this time he was re-employed, or his hours were restored, and he had enough money to fund a plan but not enough to stave off the foreclosures and repossessions.

A Chapter 13 filing is noted on a person's credit bureau report and is kept there for seven years. However, unlike a Chapter 7, a person could reestablish his credit more quickly after a 13 filing since he's repaying his debts. When the pendulum swings the other way, as it inevitably does, a person often falls back into old habits and starts to build up debt again, until the next cycle catches him flat footed in another few years. It seemed to me that a bankruptcy lawyer would always be busy.

Chapter 25
The Business of Bankruptcy

Aside from having streamlined the Chapter 13 practice, Gary was innovative in other ways. He started printing his own forms for filing Chapter 13 cases. They were accepted by the Bankruptcy courts, and he had a thriving business printing up Chapter 13 packages, with forms and worksheets, etc. He also was a pioneer in legal advertising. From 1908 until the 1977 decision by the US Supreme Court in *Bates vs. State of Arizona Bar Association*, the American Bar Association considered it unethical for lawyers to advertise, and every state bar association adopted this rule. The argument was that the practice of law was not a business, but a profession and it was considered 'beneath the dignity' of a gentleman to be so crass as to advertise his services. Advertising was grounds for immediate discipline by the state bar associations and resulted in the suspension of one's license or even disbarment. The Supreme Court held that based on the First Amendment's guarantee of the right of free speech, the Arizona Bar Association's ban on advertising 'inhibited the free flow of information and kept the public in ignorance...' However, the Court also allowed the state bar associations to draft rules reasonably regulating the type of advertising a lawyer could do. Most lawyers were wary of advertising, because of the decades of it being thought of as cheapening the profession, and because, until new rules were adopted, no one was sure what was acceptable. Gary didn't flinch. He started to advertise in Canton's newspapers and on its radio stations with catchy slogans and bold claims.

I copied his advertising in Cleveland and became one of the first lawyers to advertise there. I opened an advertising agency to take advantage of the discounts given to agencies by the media to place ads. We began with newspapers and radio stations and eventually moved on to buses and billboards and television. A secretary kept track of where a caller had seen or heard an ad so as to better spend my advertising dollars. I appeared on radio programs and TV speaking about bankruptcy and the advantages of Chapter 13. Business took off.

It says in the *Medrash Koheles Rabba* 1:34: "A person doesn't leave this world with even half of his desires fulfilled. One who has one hundred wants two hundred, and one who has two hundred wants four hundred."

I never made a conscious decision to chase after wealth, but as my practice succeeded, it seemed like the natural thing to do. This proved to be, in a manner of speaking, my undoing. It says in *Pirkei Avos*: "Who is a rich man? Someone happy with his lot." That is the ideal. Whatever I have, I'm happy with. But I also felt that if Hashem was making it easy for me to succeed maybe I shouldn't stop.

There's a well-known story about a Chassid who is complaining to his *rebbe* about his impoverished state. He can't support his family. He's depressed and wants to die. The *rebbe* scribbles an address on a piece of paper and tells him to go there and meet a man called Zusha. Zusha will give him proper advice. The Chassid gets to the address that evening. He sees a dilapidated house and he knocks on the door. A man answers.

"Are you Zusha?

"Yes. Please come in."

The house is bare of furniture except for a small broken table and a couple of broken chairs and a broken board for a bed. There are no candles for light and no food; there's no fire, and the house is freezing. It's raining and the roof is leaking. The man tells Zusha his sad story and asks what he should do?

Zusha looks at him in wonder. "You must have the wrong address. I don't know how to deal with poverty. I'm not poor and I'm very happy. *Boruch Hashem* (thank G-d), I have everything I need."

I wasn't on Zusha's *madrega* (spiritual level). I had friends who were rich, and I didn't envy them at all. I knew that rich *frum* people had no *menuchah* (no rest). They were invited to be on the board of every *shul* and school and charitable organization; *mushalachim* (beggars or fundraisers) asking for money would constantly be knocking at their doors, interrupting their dinner and their learning and their work; they were expected to give more than they could afford because most people overestimate what a rich person has in his bank account. I didn't want that kind of life. I liked to live a quiet life with nobody bothering me. I wasn't a show-off and certainly didn't want to be one. But maybe it was the American dream. I had read every Horatio Alger book when I was a kid. The idea of accumulating wealth appealed to me, even if the lifestyle didn't.

I needed a new car. My Alfa Romeo, which saw me through law school, was now almost beyond repair. It wasn't really suited for the cold and snowy Cleveland weather. It often wouldn't start on cold January mornings with the temperature below zero. It was also constantly in the shop. I could never find a truly competent foreign car mechanic in Cleveland for it. I had my mother's old 1963 Chrysler 300, which was an amazingly reliable car. But, now in 1979, at the age of sixteen, it's body and undercarriage were rusting away from all the salt on Cleveland's roads. It was time for a replacement. I thought about a new Olds 98, which was the Oldsmobile luxury model. It was a large car, about the size of a Cadillac, but not as ostentatious. Gas was cheap so that wasn't a consideration. I could buy the Olds for a fraction of my month's earnings, so cost wasn't a factor. But it looked luxurious. I didn't know if it was proper for a religious Jew to drive such a car. I didn't want to look showy. I asked my rabbi. He told me that I could buy it but without fancy hubcaps. I also bought a new Volvo station wagon for my wife after she gave birth to our baby, Miriam. Again, the expense wasn't even a month's income. It was a weird feeling to be able to basically buy whatever I needed without thinking of the cost. During law school, even though my wife had a job as a lettering artist at The American Greetings Corporation, we still needed food stamps to live. Now I felt as rich as Rockefeller. Well, not quite, but almost.

Gary and I franchised our practice. I had a number of friends who were lawyers in other cities, and we taught them our methods and got a percentage of their business for a certain period of time. Then, I got the idea to go BIG. I was going to New York at least once a month to visit my mother, who was now in a nursing home on Long Island. Why not try to break into the New York market? We bought New York newspapers and didn't see any Chapter 13 ads.

Gary and I went to New York for a closer look at the

Chapter 13 market. We visited the various Federal courthouses in four of the five boroughs and found, to our great surprise, that while there were many Chapter 7 cases, being filed, there were only a handful of 13s. Here was a gold mine. All we had to do was stake our claim. The greater Cleveland Metropolitan area had about 1.5 million people — New York had over twenty-five times that. But how could we manage it? Neither of us was willing to move to New York. Then I had a "brilliant" idea. Why not partner with an existing law firm who we could work with. I contacted my cousin who I once worked for during college. His firm was now the biggest in Suffolk County. And he was family. I could trust him. Or so I thought. He was interested in seeing our advertising and our method of handling cases. I sent him examples of everything. Naively, I didn't ask him to sign a non-disclosure agreement because I thought he would consider it offensive that I didn't trust him. I asked him if he'd like to partner with us. About a week later he told me that his partner nixed the idea. A month later, Gary showed me a copy of the *New York Daily News*. In it was our ad to stop foreclosures with the name of my cousin's law firm. He had jumped our claim to the gold mine. I was incensed. I didn't speak to him for the next twenty years.

To my mind there was nothing for us to do but to go into competition. I contacted an old friend of mine in New York, a lawyer who was now underemployed and asked her if she'd be interested in managing our offices. We went to New York and met with potential associates to man the offices in four of the five boroughs (we skipped Staten Island) and Nassau County. We hired ten young lawyers to staff the offices and set about to rent office space and equip them. The lawyers were all religious Jews with one exception, a Conservative Jew. And we began to advertise.

Advertising in New York was not like Cleveland. To run a small daily ad in the *Daily News* cost about thirty thousand dollars a month. The offices weren't cheap. We were paying salaries to ten lawyers and one managing partner and their secretaries. We hired an accountant to make sure no one was stealing from us. It was a giant gamble, but the upside was almost limitless. And I was extremely confident. I was going to be the next Horatio Alger success story. Cases started to come in, but not at the pace we had anticipated. There was almost no cash flow, we weren't generating other business. We couldn't understand why. I thought that maybe people in New York were different from Mid-Westerners. Maybe they didn't care about repaying their creditors? Maybe we weren't getting personal injury and worker's compensation cases because we were competing with major PI and worker's comp firms who could outspend us in advertising for that work. We thought it was just a matter of time until the Chapter 13 filings picked up and we would be getting monthly checks from the Trustees on our cases.

Looking back on it, it really was like the gold rush in the Wild West. If you didn't watch your back someone would shoot you in it. After a while it became clear to us that almost everyone on our payroll was stealing from us, from the managing partner down to the secretaries. The associates all had other jobs or their own practices. Since we weren't there to supervise them, they did as they pleased and got a paycheck for it. I couldn't believe it. One associate who manned our office in Brooklyn told us that he needed four hundred dollars for a deposit on a telephone line. After firing him because he filed no cases, we discovered that the office we rented for him already had a phone installed and we didn't have to pay the deposit. I asked Mendel.

"Why did you tell us that you needed four hundred dollars for a telephone deposit?"

"Well, I needed the money."

"Yes, but you stole the money, Mendel. And you lied to us."

"No, I didn't steal it, I just borrowed it."

"What about taking a salary from us without working for it? "

"I had this case in Queens that I was working on before I started working for you and I needed to finish it. It took up all of my time. I was planning to start working on our business after I finished."

"But that's called 'stealing', Don't you know that the Torah says that it's forbidden to steal?"

I was dumbfounded. I was so naïve. I had been religious for six years now and my total experience with doing business with *frum* Jews had been with Gary, who was also a *baal teshuva* (a returnee to Halachic Judaism). I assumed that all religious Jews were careful about the laws in the Torah and were all scrupulously honest in business. What bothered me much more was that Mendel showed no remorse. I couldn't understand it. Even if someone sinned, he should feel embarrassed after being caught and try to do *teshuvah* (repent). Mendel wasn't bothered at all.

It turned out that every religious lawyer had another job and spent very little time working for us. Even the managing partner, someone I thought I knew very well, was writing checks for her own personal expenses and was paying people 'off the books' with our money. The accountant was incompetent and although he gave us nice looking reports every month, he did nothing for his money.

We fired everyone but the Conservative Jew who was a very good lawyer and a hard worker. I learned a very important lesson. The fact that someone is *frum* doesn't mean he's not *krum* (crooked). It was a very expensive lesson.

But it was not the only lesson. After about a year of trying to meet with the Chapter 13 Trustees to discuss disbursements we got a call from our remaining lawyer telling us that the Brooklyn Chapter 13 Trustee had committed suicide. He hadn't shown up in court for a few days and he didn't answer his office phone. His wife and family had no idea where he was. The door to his office was locked. When the police finally broke down the door, they found him with a revolver in his hand and a hole in his head surrounded — floor to ceiling — with checks from employers of Chapter 13 clients. He had no idea how to handle the volume and had been too stubborn to listen to numerous suggestions to use the guy in Kansas City to help administer the cases. The other Trustees, although not dead, also had holes in their heads and couldn't figure out how to administer the cases and also suffered from the same *hubris* that prevented them from seeking help.

I had sunk basically all my savings into our New York venture and lost it all. But at least I wasn't in debt and still had my Cleveland practice. I was not going to be the subject of a Horatio Alger story, or one of Fortune's four hundred richest people in America. But, at least, I wasn't going to be my firm's own client.

Chapter 26
My Criminal Law Career

As I mentioned earlier, during my years of practice I have seen a number of criminal lawyers in action. I have referred cases to them and, occasionally, co-counseled with them on cases involving my clients who were in bankruptcy proceedings.

One morning, in the early 1980s, I got a frantic call from Richard Moore, a former client of mine in a bankruptcy proceeding. He wanted to see me as soon as possible. He and his wife, Carol and their twelve-year-old son, Wally, came to my office in downtown Cleveland that afternoon. Social Services in Lake County, a county to the east of Cleveland's Cuyahoga County had told the Moores that their son would be put in foster care, claiming that he had suffered physical abuse by my client, who was his stepfather. There was to be a hearing in Lake County Court in two weeks to determine if the county was justified in removing him from the home.

Richard had a steady job as a salesman in a furniture store in Mentor, Ohio. He was about thirty-five, tall, good-looking with blond hair and bright blue eyes. He dressed neatly and was friendly, engaging and intelligent. He was an excellent salesman and according to his wife and son, he was a great husband and dad. Strangely enough, he was also illiterate. He had come from a poor farming family in northeast Pennsylvania and had never gone to school. As happened often in my practice I was surprised by people, their education (or lack thereof) and lifestyles that did not conform to my previously held assumptions. I could hardly believe that in the US a person of approximately my age and who was white and of above average intelligence, was illiterate. But there he was.

Richard married Carol a year after her previous husband abandoned her and their three-month old baby, Wally. Richard was the only father Wally had ever known, and from what I heard, they loved each other like any father and son. I asked to speak to Wally alone.

"Tell me about your father, Wally? What's he like?"

"He's a great dad. We go fishing together; we play catch; we go on trips to the state parks; we fix stuff around the house. He takes us to a restaurant every Sunday. I love him."

"Does he hit you?"

"No, sir. He yells at me when I misbehave, but that's about it."

"I see you have a black eye. How did that happen?"

"A baseball — hit me in the face while we were playing in school."

"Did you speak to a Bonny Adair, the county social worker, about your father?"

"Yeah, she came to the house and asked me questions about my dad."

"What did you tell her?"

"I told her what I told you."

"Did she ask you if he hit you?"

"Yes."

"What did you say? "

"I told her — no."

Then he said:

"Mr Semenov, I'm really scared. I don't want to be taken away. I love my mom and dad. I love my little sister. Please help me."

That got me. I had to do everything to keep this family together.

I called Richard and Carol back into my office.

"Who do you think called Social Services?"

"There's this old lady who lives across the street who's always screaming at us to be quiet. She yells at the kids. She yells at us. She's the kind of neighbor that if your baseball goes onto her lawn, she won't give it back. She's mean. I would guess it was her."

I told Richard that I had never handled a case like this before and that he might want a different lawyer. I could ask around and find someone who does this kind of work.

Richard insisted that I represent them. I agreed.

The first thing I did was to call a friend who practiced family law and asked him what I should do. He suggested that I get Richard and his family an appointment with a psychologist who could write a report for the court about the family dynamics and how taking Wally from the family would have a terribly detrimental effect on him and on the family. I found a psychologist with court experience and sent the family to her. She called me back after the session.

"Richard is a diamond in the rough," she told me. "He's a loving husband and great father. I'll be happy to write a report for the court."

On the hearing date I drove out to Lake County and spoke to my clients, encouraging them to keep their hopes up and that we had a good chance of winning. The clerk called us into the courtroom and Bonny Adair, the social worker, took the stand. She described her interview with Wally and testified that he had told her that Richard had hit him. She also read a statement from an anonymous accuser who claimed that Richard hit his son and was loud and bullying; and that the home was a danger to Wally, and he should be put in foster care. I asked the social worker who gave the statement.

She answered that the author was anonymous, and she couldn't divulge the name. I asked her if it was the lady across the street. She repeated that she was not required by law to divulge the name. Turning to the judge I said that I found it incredible that the State could use a statement from an anonymous accuser, who could not be subject to cross-examination, and a child could lose his home and parents, their child, without any chance to challenge the accuser. This should be unthinkable in America.

The judge called a half hour recess. In the hallway outside the courtroom, I had a chance to chat with the social worker.

"Bonny, do you really think you're doing a favor to this boy by taking him out of his family and putting him in a foster home that may be only interested in the money the county gives them?"

"Yes," she answered.

"Would you agree that even if Richard hit his son, that's not so terrible if he did it with love. I mean parents do hit kids from time to time — sometimes for discipline or sometimes even out of frustration; but is that a reason to break up a family?"

"Yes, it is."

"What about yelling at a kid? Do you think that's reason enough to remove the kid from a family?"

"Yes. Even yelling."

After the recess we went back into the court. I asked the judge if I could approach the bench with the social worker. He agreed. I told the judge that I had just had a conversation with Bonny in the hallway and that she told me that even yelling at a kid is reason enough to remove him from the family. The judge asked Bonny if that was true. "Yes," she answered.

The judge banged the gavel on the bench and said, "I'm dismissing this case."

Justice was done.

On another occasion I had a glimpse into a world that I had only read about in newspapers and seen in movies — the world of bars. Growing up in Long Beach and Rockville Centre, and living in the Jewish world of Cleveland Heights, I didn't know any alcoholics — at least none I knew to be so. As a law student, my wife and I had gone out to bars for a few beers on Saturday night with my best friend in law school, Bob Santore and his wife, but we never got really drunk and didn't see outrageously drunken people. As a bankruptcy lawyer, I got to see another side of life. One of my clients, Dan, was a Cleveland firefighter. As were many firefighters, he was Irish. Dan also owned a bar on the west side of town. There had been a fracas at the bar one evening and he was arrested for the assault on a woman customer — Sandy.

Dan asked me to represent him in the criminal case. I told him I wasn't a criminal lawyer, but I would partner with a friend of mine, a former study partner in Law School, Dave Randall, who over the years had become an excellent criminal defense lawyer.

I was now introduced to the world of bar culture. In

Cleveland at the time, each bar was like a social club. The members were, almost to a man (or woman), serious alcoholics. What's a serious alcoholic? City law allowed bars to open from five a.m. to two a.m. There was a mandatory closing time from two a.m. to five a.m. Most of the patrons planned their day around those hours. They were there for the opening and for the closing. They worked or did other things to make money during some hours of the day, but most of those twenty-one hours were spent in the bar.

One of the witnesses at the trial, a guy about forty, whose name was Raymond, worked for the Federal Reserve Bank of Cleveland. I don't know what his position was, but he was some kind of clerk. He would be at the bar at five a.m. for opening and then leave at eight am, go to the bank and punch in; be at his desk for a couple of hours; go back to the bar and stay until four, return to the bank and punch out at five p.m. Then, of course, he would go back to the bar until closing time. I believe he was married and had a family. How he managed his life, I have no idea.

The bar was like a family. The patrons did everything together. They had baseball teams and picnics and spent almost all their waking hours together in the bar. As with many families, there are occasional squabbles. However, unlike many families, everyone in the bar was an adult and none were in total control of their words or actions.

Sandy was what I guess one could call a 'bar floozy'. She must have been quite a beauty when she was younger. She was tall, blonde and looked like the Cheerleader for the Cleveland Browns that she claimed to have been. She was also loud and violent. She claimed to have relationships with famous football players on the team. She had a German Shepherd that she would bring to the bar and feed beer. Dan would yell at her to get the dog out of the bar, but she wouldn't listen.

One day he admonished her again for bringing the dog into the bar. She responded by throwing a heavy glass ashtray at his head. It appears from the account that we were able to reconstruct, that at this point Sandy either lost her balance and fell to the floor or that Dan punched her, and they both fell to the floor. What followed was a drunken brawl during which Dan's thick eyeglasses flew off his head and were broken and Sandy at some point left the bar and went to the nearby police station to swear out a complaint against Dan. No one was seriously hurt, but Dan's liquor license was in jeopardy.

The trial opened and the prosecution's witnesses were trotted out by the young prosecutor, a Kevin McGinty. Other than a fight involving Sandy and Dan, no one seemed to remember the details, since everyone was drunk. Dave did a great job on cross-examination, and he utterly destroyed Sandy's credibility.

Dan took the stand in his own defense, which was that Sandy had initiated the fight by punching him in the face. He testified that he was just acting in self-defense. In a criminal trial the burden of proof is on the State to prove beyond a reasonable doubt that the defendant committed the crime. If the defendant's lawyer thinks that the State had failed to do that, it's dangerous to have the defendant testify since his credibility could be destroyed on cross-examination. However, Dan was insistent. He felt his reputation was at stake and wanted a chance to vindicate himself.

If the gift of the gab is given to the Irish either because of a special gene or as a result of kissing the Blarney Stone, Dan had an abundance of 'gab genes' and had probably kissed the

Blarney Stone a hundred times. He was magnificent.

The prosecutor asked him how he could tell that it was Sandy that had punched him when he was on the floor, and he wasn't wearing his glasses.

"Well, Mr McGinty, Dan answered. Let me ask you a question. Were you ever in a fire?"

"No," McGinty answered, violating an elementary maxim of trial — a cross-examining lawyer should never answer a question from a witness, except to clarify or repeat the lawyer's question.

Dan seized the opportunity.

"Thank G-d for that and may you and your loved ones never have such a tragedy befall you."

"I'm a firefighter, and as anyone knows, when you're in a house that's on fire there's no point in wearing glasses. Your face is covered in a mask and the smoke is so thick you can't see your fingers in front of your face. I'm down on my hands and knees feeling around for a baby or little child who might be hiding under the bed. No, Mr McGinty you can't see a thing, but you know what's going on. Sandy threw the ashtray at me and punched me in the face. I know that."

That was the last question McGinty asked.

The jury was out for about fifteen minutes. Dan was acquitted.

The whole gang was standing around Dan when we were called back into the courtroom for the verdict. They were all comrades again, even Sandy.

On a few occasions I had Chapter 13 clients who, unbeknownst to me, had been involved in criminal activities, which only came out during the bankruptcy proceedings.

Homer Marshall came to my office with his wife, Dolly.

They were in debt and wanted to save their house and also wanted to repay their creditors. Homer said he worked at a nearby General Motors plant for the last twenty-five years and had a steady income. I started the interview with the usual questions about names and home address, date of birth. Homer told me that he was born in 1933, which would have made him fifty years old. Dolly was born in 1934 and looked her age. I remarked to Homer that had he asked me to guess his age, I would have said 'twenty-five'. "It's remarkable how young you look."

"Yes," Homer answered, "a lot of people tell me that." I filed the case a few days later.

The debtor is required to list all his creditors in his filing and then sign, under oath, that the list is complete and true. Notices are then sent to the creditors informing them of the initial hearing date and giving them a time period to object to the plan. Most Chapter 13s receive few objections from creditors. Ours usually received none, since our plans usually paid the creditors in full, less interest and penalties. There are certain debts, which by law, can't be discharged — like taxes or child support or educational loans or debts obtained by fraud. Those must be repaid in full.

In the Marshall case we got a notice of an objection by a Mr Thomas O'Malley, the owner of a chain of gas stations in the inner-city neighborhoods of Cleveland. He claimed Homer owed him nine hundred dollars. We hadn't listed him as a creditor, and I had no idea who he was. I called Mr Marshall. He said he had no idea who he was.

When we got to the initial hearing, a very dapper looking O'Malley was there with his lawyer, O'Brian, an old-time member of the Bankruptcy bar. The lawyer asked Judge

O'Neal to put Mr Marshall on the stand.

Homer approached, stood in the witness box and was sworn in.

O'Brian began.

"Please state your name."

"Homer Marshall."

"Remember Mr Marshall, you are under oath."

"Yes sir."

"Please state your name again."

"Homer Marshall."

At this point Mr O'Malley jumps up and yells: "I know Homer Marshall, that's not him, this is Homer Marshall," as he points to an older man in the gallery sitting next to Dolly.

Judge O'Neal, looking quite stern, says to the man on the stand.

"Do you know the penalty for perjury in a court of law can be as much as five years in prison."

"But my name is Homer Marshall."

The thought went through my mind that I was watching the popular television show 'To Tell the Truth' where three people all claim to be Homer Marshall. At the end of the segment the moderator says: "Will the real Homer Marshall please stand up?"

That's not what happened.

"I'm Homer Marshall, Jr. and that other man is my father, Homer Marshall, Sr."

"Mr Semenov," the Judge asked me sharply, "which one is your client?"

I really wasn't sure. I knew that the guy on the stand was the one that came to my office, and Dolly sure looked like his mother. It was obvious that Jr. had been impersonating his father in my office and in court. I didn't really know why.

"Your Honor," I said, "the man on the stand is the one who I assumed was my client, but now it appears that the man in the gallery is really my client. I'd like to ask the court to dismiss the case."

"Not so fast," answered Judge O'Neal. "I'd like to get to the bottom of this. Mr O'Malley, please approach the bench."

O'Malley was sworn in.

The Judge proceeded to ask O'Malley questions.

"Please tell the court why you are here."

"Your Honor," O'Malley answered, "Homer Marshall, the man I pointed out to you, worked for me at my gas station on Carnegie Avenue. About two months ago he told me that the station was held up by armed robbers and about nine hundred dollars in cash was taken. There was no police report or calls to the police. I suspected that Mr Marshall had stolen the money himself and made up the story. He had no good explanation as to why he didn't call the police. I fired him but told him to repay the money and I wouldn't have him arrested. He agreed. My collection attorney noticed the Chapter 13 filing and remembered the name of my employee and told me about it."

"Mr Marshall," Judge O'Neal said sternly, "did you steal the money?"

"No sir."

"Did you agree to pay the nine hundred dollars to Mr O'Malley?"

"Yes sir."

"If it is not paid within thirty days, I will issue a warrant for your arrest. Do you understand?"

"Yes sir. Thank you, your Honor."

"Case dismissed."

I asked Homer Marshall, Jr. how he could do such a thing and mislead me?

"My father didn't want to miss work to come into the office and asked me to fill in for him." — as if this was the most normal thing in the world.

The Bankruptcy case that had the most connection to criminal activity was unquestionably the case of Edward Arnold. Edward was a tall, muscular, intelligent and very polite Black man who had recently lost his job as a maître d' in a fancy restaurant. He had fallen behind in his mortgage payments and was in danger of losing his house, where his estranged wife lived with their two children. The case was fairly straightforward, as Edward had recently found another job, whose payroll deduction could fund the plan. One of the debts listed was seven thousand dollars for back rent due on the apartment Edward was renting. The landlord was Joe Gigante. We disputed the claim and asked for a trial in Bankruptcy Court to determine the validity of the debt.

Edward told me that the job that he had lost was in a restaurant that his landlord owned and had gone out of business. At the same time, his boss disappeared. He listed the debt, even though Gigante didn't charge him for rent as long as he worked in the restaurant, but after losing his job he had gotten a letter from Gigante's attorney demanding back rent. He also told me that the restaurant was frequented by a lot of the Cleveland Mafia people and Gigante was involved with them.

A couple of weeks after filing the case, I got a request from Gigante's attorney, Marty Rothenberg, a well-known criminal defense lawyer, for a deposition of my client. Depositions are part of the pre-trial phase of a case. Normally a lawyer will request to depose the opposing party and various witnesses for the other side to find out what they plan to say at trial and what they know. He can then fact check the statements made and figure out a strategy for winning. The deposition was held in Marty's office. Gigante wasn't present. My client answered all the questions asked to him in a straightforward and seemingly truthful manner.

Then Marty asked him: "Mr Arnold, have you ever been convicted of a felony?"

I objected to the question. "This is a bankruptcy case. It's irrelevant."

"No," answered Rothenberg, if he has committed a felony then his truthfulness is called into question, so it's a material question."

In a deposition, which is usually held without a judge, but with a court reporter, the objection is made, and the witness answers the question. If the judge later sustains the objection, then both the question and answer are stricken from the transcript and cannot be used at trial.

I told Edward to answer the question.

"Yes," he answered.

"For what crime?" asked Rothenberg.

"Manslaughter."

"And did you serve prison time for your crime?"

"Yes."

"How long?"

"Five years."

"Thank you, Mr Arnold. No further questions."

As we left the office I asked Arnold, with some

apprehension, because he wasn't the person, I thought he was, whom he had killed.

"My first wife. I came home early from work one day and found her in bed with another man. I shot her on the spot. Anyone would have done the same."

I couldn't argue, I had no clue about life on another planet, even though I did recall the case of the exotic dancer that intrigued me so much when I clerked for my cousin. I guess his was a normal reaction among people with guns.

But that wasn't the end of the case and certainly not the most surprising part. A week or so later, I got a notice of a deposition for Joe Gigante from his own attorney. In my years of practice, I had never heard of a lawyer deposing his own client. I called Rothenberg.

"I don't understand," I told him. "Why would you depose your own client?"

"I want to preserve his testimony."

"Why would you do that, is he ill?"

"You never know," Rothenberg answered mysteriously.

Since Gigante was in the Mafia, I could imagine what that meant.

At his deposition, Gigante testified about his claim in the bankruptcy cases. He seemed quite friendly.

At the initial bankruptcy hearing, Gigante was not there, and we settled the claim with Rothenberg. There was no further need for a trial.

About a year later, the Plain Dealer had a lead story about Joe Gigante's disappearance, which was shortly after his deposition. Gigante was a Mafia underboss who had been given control over various coal mines in Southern Ohio and West Virginia to run for the mob. Coal mining, I guess was a lucrative business and generated other business, like drugs, prostitution and loan sharking. Apparently, Joe was not a good manager, and his books didn't balance. He was given a few warnings but didn't reform. He decided to retire to Florida, and then, with his fortunes in reverse, he lost the restaurant and disappeared.

A couple of months after that the Plain Dealer announced the arrest of Hans 'the surgeon' Schmidt. Hans was a seemingly mild-mannered pet shop owner in Cleveland who had a side business that he conducted in the basement of the pet shop. He would receive deliveries of truant mobsters or others on the mob's hit list; kill them and cut them up into small pieces with a surgeon's saw and then into smaller pieces with a scalpel and then put the pieces into a false basement wall, which he would then cover with a fresh layer of cement. Someone had obviously ratted on Hans and the police found remains of many dead men, among them Joe Gigante in the basement wall.

Chapter 27
Turning Point

As the years passed and our practice expanded, we rented larger and plusher offices and hired new lawyers, paralegals and secretaries. We now had burgeoning personal injury and Workers' Compensation departments generated from our Chapter 13 clients, and an established *mincha minyan*. I had worked very hard for a few years building up the practice and now was able to delegate most court appearances and other time-consuming activities to others. I was busy with managing the firm but had more time to devote to other pursuits. I got more involved in the Jewish community and was the only Orthodox member of the Board of the Free Loan Society of the Jewish Federation. I also was on the Board of the Telshe Yeshiva and was president of Yavne Seminary for Women. I did *pro bono* legal work for Jewish institutions in Cleveland. But as I got older, I got more restless.

I had, of course, read and heard about 'mid-life crisis'. I even had a couple of close lawyer friends, who gave up the practice of law and went into teaching. As I approached my late thirties, I also felt the need to expand my horizons and seek self-fulfillment. I wasn't unhappy practicing law. I couldn't imagine another job that would appeal to me as much. But I asked myself, "Is this all I want out of life?" A good profession? A *parnassa* (an income)? What about *ruchnius*?

What about my spiritual life? Was I growing? Fast enough?

At this point I think it would be appropriate to review my development as an Orthodox Jew. As I mentioned earlier, I had a great grandmother, Deena Rochel (Nani Nani) who had a major influence on this part of my life. Her singing to me about the Torah; her rock solid *Emunah* (faith) in Hashem; her davening and saying *Tehillim* all day long, every day, made an indelible impression on me. As someone who works in a Yeshiva for *baalei teshuva* (newly religious) and has interacted with hundreds of them over the years, I am familiar with their struggles in accepting the existence of G-d and practicing *mitzvohs*. But for me, I never had a question about the existence of G-d. It was a given.

Of course, belief in G-d is one thing. Feeling obligated to do the *mitzvohs* is another. Growing up I never had the feeling that I was doing anything wrong by not keeping Shabbos or *kashrus*. I knew Jews who did keep them and even had a good friend who did. And I thought that doing so was quaint and even respectable. That was the tradition in their families. I liked the idea of tradition. Ours included listening to the *Kiddush* Cantor Caplow made for Nani Nani on Friday night, going to *shul* on Rosh Hashanah and Yom Kippur, having a Passover *seder* and lighting Chanukah candles. These were our traditions. I never felt a need to do more.

My brother, Yaacov Meir, and some friends of mine were much more ideological in their approach. Once they were convinced that the Torah was true — that Hashem had spoken to the Jewish People on Mount Sinai and gave us rules to live by, they were immediately obligated to keep everything. I completely understand this position and think it's the only logical one. But, for some reason or other I never thought like that.

My wife's conversions, and our increasing participation in Jewish communal life and eventual observance was a slow process. I knew that the goal was to eventually keep all the *mitzvohs,* but I never felt that I had to do it all at once. I assumed that Hashem would be happy if we moved at a slow pace. And no one told us otherwise. We stopped listening to the radio on the Shabbos drive to *shul*; we stopped buying non-kosher food; we stopped eating in non-kosher restaurants and eventually stopped driving on Shabbos — everything at our slow pace.

This doesn't mean that my belief wasn't also intellectually grounded. I was struck by the astounding improbability of an evolutionary process that produced such a balanced and integrated world without a Creator. This is sometimes known as 'The Watchmaker Analogy' or 'Intelligent Design'. Some people argue that 'Intelligent Design' is not a convincing argument for a scientist. But that's not so. A friend of mine, a physics professor at Case Western Reserve University, told me that the reason he became observant was through his study of color vision. It would seem, according to evolutionary theory, that those species higher up on the evolutionary chain with larger brains relative to their body mass would develop more complex functions. Color vision, he told me, is incredibly complex and should logically require a large brain. Yet, some mollusks, other invertebrates, birds, reptiles and fish, which have small brains have tetrachromatic vision which enables them to detect ultraviolet wavelengths of light that translate in the brain to colors that are invisible to the human eye. Humans and other primates have trichromatic color vision, and most mammals have only dichromatic color vision, rendering them basically colorblind. (An article in the July 2006 issue of *Scientific American* entitled 'See' by Dr Timothy Goldsmith, an emeritus Professor of Biology at Yale University explains the intricacies of color vision). This revelation led him to the belief that there must be a Creator.

But what was most convincing to me, early on in my religious life, was the Torah itself. In Leviticus we are given laws of *tumah* and *taharah* — a plethora of rules in minute detail determining whether an object or person or food is ritually pure or impure and what is its level of purity. Purity is essential for sacrifices, for eating certain foods, for marital relations and other aspects of life. Impurity can be caused by certain physical emissions and contact with people and animals who are *tamei* (impure) or the dead or even being in certain proximity or enclosures that are impure. Removing the impurity and being restored to a state of purity has many sets of rules, depending on the level of impurity. If humans wrote the Torah, why would they make up such complicated and irrational rules? One could say, as a doctor friend of mine did when I told him of my argument. — "A highly intelligent OCD person could come up with them." Granted. But how would you convince an intelligent nation to go along with such craziness if it wasn't Divinely commanded. This argument seems to me to be unassailable.

By the time we got to Cleveland we were fully committed to keeping Shabbos and *kashrus*. We were what I would call today '*dati leumi*' or 'Modern Orthodox'. We certainly didn't relate to the 'Yeshiva' world — the world of black hats, black suits and white shirts.

Because my Hebrew reading skills at the beginning of my spiritual journey were almost non-existent, I initially didn't *daven* daily with a *minyan*. I could not keep up with the congregation. After my first year of law school, I began going to *minyan* in the morning. There was a forty-five-minute *gemara shiur* (class) before *shacharis* (morning prayers) and I started going to that too. It awakened the interest I had in learning *gemara* that had been dormant for over a year.

By the start of my third year of law school, Telshe Yeshiva had started a learning program in Cleveland Heights, where we lived. Members of the Telshe *Kollel* (the married students of the Yeshiva) would come from Wickliffe, the site of the Yeshiva, a few evenings a week, to learn with *baalei batim* (working people). I had a few tutors. My first one was Izzy Schmeltzer. He was a great teacher. We started with *Meseches Beitza*, which deals with *hilchos yom tov* (the laws of festivals). He had me memorize the *shakla v'tariya* (the stream of argument) of the *sugya* (the topic) we were learning and would test me on it the next time we met. It was a very rigorous approach to learning *gemara* and one that appealed to me. I felt I was making progress. After about a year I could see myself, in the far distant future, as actually reaching a level where I might be able to learn a piece of *gemara* on my own.

After two years of learning I completed Meseches *Beitzah* and made a *siyum* (a festive meal celebrating the completion of a tractate). I felt good about myself, but also realized how handicapped I really was. If I was ever to get to a level of others my age who had learnt in yeshiva, I would have to 'up my game'. I needed to learn more. At about this time, the Telshe *Rosh HaYeshiva (the head of the Yeshiva)*, Rav Mordechai Gifter, started coming to the Heights on Sunday mornings to teach the *Sefer HaChinuch* (The Book of the Mitzvohs). As Rav Gifter was wont to often quote the anonymous author of this thirteenth century work (who describes himself only as a "Levite from Barcelona."), the purpose of this book is to give us *taamei hamitzvohs* — 'the taste' of the *mitzvohs*. Rav Gifter emphasized that to give a 'reason' for a *mitzvoh* is impossible, because we have no way of divining the mind of the Divinity. We can only experience a 'taste' — an insight into the *mitzvoh* that we, on our level, can understand. I cannot describe the impact this man made on me. He spoke to my heart. Rav Gifter was born in Richmond, Virginia and never lost the slight trace of a Southern accent. He was a brilliant orator. I am sure that had he decided to go into politics instead of the rabbinate, he would have been the most eloquent Senator in the US Congress. I can still hear his stentorian voice exclaiming, "If we believe there is a Commander, then we must follow His command." This experience of hearing Rav Gifter's voice is not only my own. Almost anyone who heard him years ago can still hear him now.

When my law practice had reached the point where I could take some more time off, I made up my mind to spend a couple of hours every day in the Yeshiva, which was about a twenty-minute drive from my office. I planned to leave work at about 4:00 p.m. and learn in the Yeshiva until 6:15 p.m. I told my partners about my decision, and they reluctantly accepted it. Since I had started the firm, I felt I had a legitimate claim. I loved being in the holy atmosphere of the Yeshiva and I loved the arguments over the texts with my *chavrusah* (study partner), Aryeh Bernstein, a *baal teshuva*, like me. Aryeh had graduated from Dartmouth and was in the Navy during

Vietnam.

I did make progress, but my working life kept intruding on my learning. Even though these were the days before the Internet and cell phones, my practice occupied a significant portion of my brain, and I would often take breaks to call the office or to call a client to troubleshoot this problem or that or to prepare for a trial. I knew that for me to make real progress in my learning I would have to stop working and just learn. I was becoming *yeshivishe*.

I was also changing in other ways. Even though I knew that I might annoy people by criticizing their behavior, I felt compelled to do so anyway. I would frequently ask Jewish lawyers I met to learn with me and to come for Shabbos. I was convinced that such an experience would change their lives as it had mine. I'm sure that most of my friends considered me some kind of religious fanatic — a nice religious fanatic, but still a fanatic. And maybe I was. But it didn't stop me. And once I succeeded beyond my wildest dreams.

Brett was my age, an associate in a bankruptcy firm, but one that represented creditors. We met daily in court as opponents but developed a warm friendship. There is quite a bit of down time between cases, and we would grab a coffee and sit together for a chat. After a while, Brett opened up to me about his marriage. He grew up in Cleveland and attended a religious afternoon school, His family was traditional, although not Orthodox. He went away to college and law school and while there he met his wife, a Protestant girl from Vermont. They married and settled in Cleveland. She wasn't interested in converting and his family was accepting of her the way she was. Although he was quite happy at first, now that their twin daughters were five, Brett was feeling a bit uncomfortable knowing that his children weren't Jewish. He asked me what I thought of his situation.

"Would your wife be willing to convert?"

I didn't mention to him the fact that to do so and be universally accepted as a Jew, she would have to agree to keep all the *mitzvohs* including Shabbos and *kashrus* and that would mean that he would too. He probably knew that anyway.

"No way," he said. "I've discussed it with her. She will not convert."

"Brett," I said, "In that case, I know that what I'm going to tell you will sound crazy. But it's the only solution. You should divorce your wife and marry a Jewish woman."

He told me that it was out of the question, that he loved his wife and his girls. He wouldn't divorce.

I asked Brett to come with his family for Shabbos. Maybe after seeing the beauty of Shabbos and talking to my wife, his wife might feel differently. He declined, saying that his wife would never agree to come. But did that stop me? Of course not! I would invite him week after week. He always refused.

One Thursday in the summertime, when we were in court, I invited Brett again.

"You know what," he answered, "my wife took the kids to her parents in Vermont for two weeks. I guess I could come."

"Great," I said, "Shabbos starts at eight p.m. Come to my house about fifteen minutes before that so that we have time to get to *shul* for *davening*."

Brett showed up at a quarter to eight. He had parked his car on the street. Cleveland Heights had a safety regulation requiring all cars to be off the street and in driveways from two a.m. to six a.m. Brett also lived in Cleveland Heights.

"Brett, you know that Cleveland Heights forbids street parking overnight. Pull your car into my driveway."

"What are you talking about?" he asked, "I'm only staying for dinner."

"No," I answered. "I invited you for Shabbos. Shabbos is twenty-five hours. It's forbidden to drive on Shabbos. I thought I was quite clear about Shabbos."

"I thought that when you said, 'Shabbos' you meant Friday night."

"Oh well" he finally said resignedly, "I guess there's no harm in staying here until Saturday night."

"We'll have a great time," I said. "You'll have a real Shabbos experience."

Brett stayed and we had a lovely Shabbos with him, and he left after *Havdalah* (a ceremony concluding Shabbos).

About six months later, I was driving to my office late on a Sunday morning. As I drove by a strip mall, I saw a dejected Brett, hands in his pockets and head hanging down, walking up the street. I stopped the car and got out to say hello.

"You look sad, Brett. What's the matter?"

"Do you have a few minutes?"

"For you? As long as you want."

"Do you remember when you invited me for Shabbos?"

"Of course, I do."

"Well on that Friday evening my wife was trying to call me from Vermont. And, of course, I wasn't home because I was staying with you. "

"Yeah?"

"When she couldn't reach me, she called my parents'

house, thinking that I might be there. But of course, I wasn't. Then both she and my parents got very worried about me. My father drove over to my house where I wasn't, and the car was gone. All day Saturday they were trying to locate me. They were about to call the police when I finally got back home on Saturday night, listened to my voice messages and called my parents and my wife. She asked me where I was and told her I was with you. She didn't believe me. I told her she could call you and verify that I was telling the truth. She said, "Sure, Brett, I'm sure he'll tell me that you stayed at his house overnight. But I won't believe it."

"Things went downhill after that. When she got back to Cleveland she was as cold as ice. Nothing I could say could change her mind. A few months after that she told me that she's been seeing someone else and last night she told me she wanted a divorce. I've been heartsick and haven't slept for two nights. I don't know what to do."

I felt sorry for Brett and for the pain he was going through. And I let him know that I was always there for him.

About four months after this episode, I noticed that Brett, who I saw almost every day in court, looked a bit more chipper. I asked him how things were going with him.

"You'll never believe this," he said, but I've been seeing someone seriously for the last month and we're planning to get married.

"Is she Jewish?" I asked.

"Yes. She's a girl from Cleveland, I know her father well. He's a prominent lawyer in town. She's also divorced."

Brett and Jackie were very happy together. In addition to Jackie's five children from her previous marriage, they had three more. Brett often told me:

"You know that I have you to thank for my life. If you hadn't invited me that Shabbos and insisted on me staying overnight, none of this would have happened."

I told him that it wasn't me, but it was the hand of Hashem.

I used my advantage to try to get Brett and Jackie to become more traditional. They started lighting candles every Friday night and had *Kiddush* and a Shabbos meal. Brett asked me to get him *tefillin* (ritual objects worn while *davening shacharis*), which I did. He put them on daily and said the *Shema* prayer. I'd like to say that they became Orthodox, but that didn't happen. As the *gemara* says: "*Tafasta merubah lo tasfasta, tafasta meutah tefasta.*" If you try for too much you won't get anywhere, but if you try for a little you can get somewhere.

Chapter 28
The Big Move

We were members of Young Israel of Cleveland on Taylor Road in Cleveland Heights (there was another branch of Young Israel in University Heights). The Rabbi was Rabbi Schubert Spero. He was (and still is, *bli ayin hara*) a wonderful and inspiring speaker and a brilliant man. Apart from being our rabbi he was also a philosophy professor at Case Western Reserve University. Rabbi Spero was an ardent religious Zionist. This was unusual for someone with his yeshiva background. He was not a Yeshiva University graduate — a decidedly Zionistic institution, but an alumnus of Yeshivas Torah v'Daas, a traditional right-wing yeshiva in Brooklyn. The Spero family was among the founders of the Orthodox Jewish community in Cleveland, arriving there in the 1880s and probably the only immigrant family to Cleveland from that time that remained Orthodox.

He encouraged *aliyah* (settling in Israel) in almost every Shabbos *drasha* (speech). It was not just some messianic dream, but something very compelling and practical. Most of our friends, the young people in the *shul*, considered *aliyah* very seriously. When a Jewish Agency *shaliach* (agent) came to town we, along with many friends, attended regular meetings with him and his wife. They discussed the practical aspects of making *aliyah* — what you should bring with you on your lift (the shipping container allowed to come in without import duties); schooling for children; neighborhoods; etc. etc. Many of our closest friends began making *aliyah* and many followed. Rabbi Spero and his children, all married by now, preceded or followed him within a short period of time.

Our decision to make *aliyah* was influenced by him and by a number of other factors. Although I was spending more time at the Telshe Yeshiva and less at work, I felt the burden of the practice weighing down on my ability to progress in my learning. If I really wanted to obtain mastery in Torah learning, I knew it couldn't be done in my spare time. I would have to devote full time to it for a number of years. My absence from the office was grating on my partners and I didn't think I could carry on with my schedule without a showdown. Although moving to Israel would mean giving up my practice and my life in America, I was ready for it. My wife, who was always more interested in the spiritual life than the material one, was enthusiastic. She also never felt totally comfortable in the US. She was a European city girl and missed living in a place with lots of people on the street and cafes everywhere. Cleveland Heights was definitely not like that. It was a suburb, and socializing was done by appointment. No one walked anywhere, except on Shabbos. It was a boring place for her.

Now that I was *yeshivishe* I felt I needed the approval of my *Rosh HaYeshiva*, Rav Gifter, whom I had grown increasingly fond of. He had moved to Israel for a number of years to open and head a branch of Telshe Yeshiva in Telshe Stone — on land, which was purchased by the great Cleveland philanthropist, Irving Stone, my wife's former boss. While Rabbi Spero was an inspiring and enthusiastic Zionist, and based his arguments on *halacha* and the Prophets, Rabbi Gifter was a poetic Zionist. He had a burning love for the Land. When his co-*Rosh HaYeshiva*, Rav Boruch Sorotzkin, who had remained in Cleveland, died, the Yeshiva family asked him to return to Cleveland and resume his leadership there. He didn't want to go, but he felt the decision wasn't his alone to make. He asked the *Godol Hador* (the greatest rabbi of the generation), The Steipler Rov — the leader of the Lithuanian Yeshivos in Israel what he should do. The Steipler told him that he had to return. The leadership of the Telshe Yeshiva had precedence over Rav Gifter's personal reasons for staying in the Holy Land. He cried. He didn't want to go back, but what could he do, *Daas Torah* (the voice of the Torah) had spoken.

Although he returned, he could never reconcile himself to living in *Chutz L'aretz* (the world outside of Israel). He refused to live in the house built for him on Yeshiva Lane but moved with his wife into the student dormitory. I visited with him there on a number of occasions. He had preserved flowers indigenous to *Eretz Yisroel* and kept them on prominent display in the dining room area. He showed them to every visitor and waxed poetic about the red and purple *kalanit* and *rakefet*. He told me that he encouraged the *bochurim* (unmarried students) at the Yeshiva in Telshe Stone to accompany him on his half hour daily stroll after *shacharis* through the forests of the settlement, pointing out the different flora and fauna as he spoke to them about the beauty of *Eretz Yisroel*. Once, upon returning to Wickliffe after a winter vacation in Miami Beach, he was shocked to find carpeting on the floor of his apartment in the dorm. Some well-meaning alumni thought to make his dorm rooms cozier and had the carpet installed while he was gone. He ordered it removed immediately, saying:

"What were they thinking? If I wanted to live in a dwelling with carpeting I would have moved back to my house. I live in the dorm because I can't live in a *diras kevah* (a permanent house) in *chutz l'aretz*, only in Eretz Yisroel. This is a *diras aray* (a temporary dwelling). And a *diras aray* doesn't have carpeting. "

Rav Gifter's love of *Eretz Yisroel* was infectious and spoke to my heart. However, he was also realistic and insisted that I have a realistic plan before I go. He told me that I needed a certain amount of money — enough to buy an apartment and sustain the family while I learnt. But he was very encouraging of the idea of my going to learn in yeshiva.

After the fiasco in New York, I needed to wait and build up my bank account before I could leave. At this point Miraim was seven and Rochi was three. He also didn't think we could delay much longer because of the issues of social integration of our girls, particularly Miriam, into the cliquish Israeli *haredi* (ultra-orthodox) society.

We decided we would be able to move within about a year and applied to make *aliyah*. In November of 1986, our son, Binyamin Tzvi was born. We made *aliyah* before his first birthday.

But before doing so I had to try to sell my interest in the law practice to my partners. That was not a given. The value of a partnership minus the managing partner is not a simple calculation. I got no argument about the accounts receivable. Since the work on those cases had already been finished there was no reason that I shouldn't share equally in those accounts. The problem arose with cases that were in the office, but not yet completed and with cases that had not yet come to us but would come based on the reputation of the firm with my name on it. This 'good will' also has a value. Determining a formula for the buyout was complicated. Fortunately for me, my partners were Mid-Westerners and believed in fairness. In the end we reached an amicable settlement that none of us was one hundred percent happy with, but we all recognized as fair. It enabled me to come to *Eretz Yisroel* with a nest egg to meet our financial needs for a number of years without needing to work. I would now be a *Kollel* man.

Epilogue

In June of 2021, a distant cousin of ours, Joshua Benghiat, contacted my brother through a genealogical website. It seems that our common great-great maternal grandmother, Rosa Furman, had immigrated to the United States in 1899; approximately three years after my great-grandmother had come to New York with her children to be reunited with her husband, my great-grandfather, who had preceded them. Joshua had located census information, her death certificate and her grave in the Baron Hirsch Cemetery on Staten Island.

Rosa Furman's tombstone. Baron Hirsch Cemetery. Staten Island, NY. 2021.

She died at home in the Bronx on May 9, 1915, at the age of sixty-eight. (Curiously, her *Yahrzeit* (the date of her death) is on the same day as my mother's, the 25th of Iyar according to the Hebrew calendar). We had always assumed that she had stayed in Bucharest. The three of us, Josh, Yaacov Meir and myself, met at the cemetery and after prayers at the gravesite retired to a nearby kosher restaurant to get acquainted. It was a memorable experience that we hope to repeat.

My brother, after some investigation and conversations with another cousin heard the following story:

Our great-grandmother, Rosa the daughter of Binyamin Zev, had married a fur dealer with the eponymous last name of Furman. Papa Furman was a modestly successful merchant but had aspirations for greater prosperity. To be closer to the source of his merchandise and avoid costly middlemen, he declared his intention to move to Siberia. His children, whom, I believe, were all married with children, chose to move to America, which they did in 1896. Rosa resisted the move and the couple remained in Bucharest for a few years afterwards. She had no interest in moving to what was generally considered to be a frozen hell on earth. She also greatly missed her children. Somehow (probably by claiming that her husband was almost out of his mind for his choice of domicile) she managed to convince the rabbis of Bucharest to force her husband to divorce her. She made her way to New York and happily lived the last sixteen years of her life in the company of her children and extended family. We don't know what happened to Papa Furman. Did he move to Siberia? Did he stay in Bucharest? Did he remarry? Do we have other missing relatives? Perhaps one day we'll find out.

Glossary

All words in the Glossary are Hebrew words, except where otherwise noted.

A'h — *Olov Hashalom* or *Olaha Hashalom*. — May he (she) rest in peace.
Aliyah n. — Immigration to Israel.
Am Kishe Oref — A stiff necked people.
Aybishter n. — The Lord.

Baal Teshuvah n. A repentant Jew.
Baalei Batim n. Working men.
Bas n. — Daughter.
Beis Medrash n. — Study Hall.
Bli Eyin Hara — The evil eye should have no power.

Chanukah n. — The Winter festival of Lights.
Chassidim n. — Followers of a Chassidic Rabbi.

Chuppah n. — Wedding canopy. Sometimes used to mean wedding.
Chutz l'Aretz n. — All land outside of Israel.

Daven v. — To pray.
Da'as Torah n. — The wisdom of the Torah.
Dati Leumi n. — Nationalist-Religious.

Dina d'Malchusa — The law of the Land.
Drasha n. — A speech about a Torah topic.

Ezer C'negdo n. — Helpmate.

Freir n. — A simpleton or idiot.
Frum adj. — Religious.

Gemara n. — A book of the Talmud.
Godol Hador n. — The greatest Torah Scholar in the generation.
Goy n. — A non-Jew.
Goyishe adj. — In a non-Jewish way.

Halacha n. - Jewish law.
Hashem n. — The Lord.
Heimishe adj. — Homelike or familiar.
Heter Iska n. — An agreement between parties that restructures debt as a loan plus an investment.

Kaddish n. — A prayer said for the dead.
Kashrus n. — Laws of Kosher Food.
Kesuba n. — A Jewish marriage contract.
Kiruv n. — Bringing someone closer to Torah observance.
Kiruv Rechokim — Bringing those far away from Torah closer.
Kollel n. - An institute for Married Students of Torah.

Litvak n. Someone whose family came from Lithuania.
L'shana Haba B'Yerushalayim — Next year in Jerusalem.

Mechitzah n. — A wall separating men from women in a shul.

Melamed n. — A teacher.
Menorah n. — A ritual lamp used on Chanukah.
Meseches n. — A tractate of the Oral Law.
Minyan n. — A prayer quorem.
Mitzvoh n. — A commandment.

Parsha n. — The Torah portion of the week.
Payos n. — Sidelocks.

Rabbeim n. — Rabbis.
Rachmonos n. — Pity or Mercy.
Refuah Shleima — Get well.
Rishonim n. — Early Torah Authorities. Generally, from 1000 CE.
To 1500 CE.
Rosh Hashana n. — The Festival of the New Year.
Rosh HaYeshiva n. — Head of a Yeshiva.

Seder n. — A session in a Yeshiva. As in Morning Seder or Afternoon Seder.
Sefer n. — Book.
Shabbos n. — Sabbath.
Shaliach n. — An agent.

Shakla v'Tariya — A flow of argument in a Gemara.
Shema Yisroel n. — Prayer declaring the Unity of the Lord.
Shetetl n. — A Jewish town usually in Eastern Europe.
Shochet n. — A ritual slaughterer.
Shomer Shabbos n. — One who keeps the laws of Shabbos.
Shul n. — Synagogue.
Siayata D'Shmaya. — With the help of Heaven.

Siddur n. — *A prayer book.*
Siyum n. — *A party made upon the completion of a tractate of Gemara.*
Sugya n. — *A topic discussed in a Gemara.*

Tahara — *Ritual cleanliness.*
Talmid n. — *A Torah student.*
Talmud n. — *The Oral Law.*
Tehillim n. — *Psalms.*
Tumah n. — *Ritual uncleanliness.*
Taam n. — *Taste.*
Tzadik or Tzadekes n. — *A male or female righteous person.*
Trief n. — *Not kosher.*

Yeshiva n. — *A Jewish learning institution.*
Yarmulka n. — *A skullcap.*

Z'l — *Zechair Tzadik L'Bracha. The memory of Righteous should be a blessing.*

Aybishter n. — *The Lord. Yiddish.*
Daven v. — *To pray. Yiddish.*
Dina d'malchusa — Aramaic.
Freir — Yiddish.
Heimishe — Yiddish.
Heter Iska — Aramaic.
Shakla v'Tariya —Aramaic.
Shtetl — Yiddish. (also note change in spelling)
Shul —Yiddish.
Siyata D'Shmaya — Aramaic.
Yarmulke — Yiddish.